English for Hospitality and Tourism

Preface

The most important features of this book are :

- It is a practical English book for hospitality and tourism service industry. It deals only with practical hospitality and tourism conversation and is not a general English course book.
- It is a book for college students.
- It can be used for primary classroom text or supplementary course material.

There are 13 units in the book, and each unit is about a different situation of Hospitality & Tourism Service Industry. Units are not ordered according to difficulty and should therefore be selected and used in the order appropriate for you. The book should not be worked through from beginning to end. For example, if you want to know the airline check-in counter, use the contents to find the unit you need to study. The units are listed in the Contents.

You can use the book in this way :

1. Look in the Contents to find the unit that you need.

2. Study the words and phrases.
3. Do the dialog and exercise.
4. Do the discussion with co-workers.
5. Study the reading.

Do not forget the reading at the back of the unit. These will give you various information about tourism industry.

This text can improve your understanding of the practical English for hospitality and tourism and provide the necessary skills to survive in the tourism industry. However, skills and practical tourism English alone will not make you successful; A solid basic knowledge of the English is a must in becoming a successful tourism service provider. Therefore, do not forget the general study of the English language as you work to prepare for tourism industry.

We would like to thank Jongwook Kim, and Wooksang Jin for their help in producing this book.

Contents

Unit 01

I'd like to make a reservation for a flight to New York.

01 *I'd like to make a reservation for a flight to New York.*

Before we go

- Do you like traveling?
- Do you prefer to travel by plane, train or automobile?

Words and phrases

- make a reservation
- just a moment
- cancellation
- flight
- economy(coach)/business/first class
- payment
- one-way/round trip
- itinerary

Flight reservation

CD TRACK 1

Chae-rim :	Hello, is this Smile Airlines reservations?
Reservation clerk :	Yes, ma'am. How may I help you?
Chae-rim :	**I'd like to make a reservation** for a flight from Seoul to New York.
Reservation clerk :	When would you like the reservation for?
Chae-rim :	July 20th, if possible.
Reservation clerk :	Just a moment, please. Will you be flying economy, business or first class?
Chae-rim :	Economy, please.
Reservation clerk :	Will you be flying one-way or round trip?
Chae-rim :	Round trip, please.
Reservation clerk :	When would you like to return?
Chae-rim :	The 2nd of August.
Reservation clerk :	**Let me check** if seats are available... **Thank you for waiting.** I found a seat for you. Can I have your name please?
Chae-rim :	My name is Chae-rim Lee. Lee is my last name.
Reservation clerk :	Okay, here is your flight itinerary. You leave

	for New York at 8:00 pm on the 20th of July and return to Seoul on the 2nd of August on our 3:10 pm flight. How about that?
Chae-rim :	That's fine.
Reservation clerk :	This is your confirmation number. It's 520-0698. If you need any help or have any questions, please call 800-520-0698. Have a nice day!
Chae-rim :	Thank you! You too. Good bye.

Change reservation

CD TRACK 2

Reservation clerk :	Good afternoon, this is Smile Airlines reservation. May I help you?
Chae-rim :	Hi, I want to change my flight schedule, please.
Reservation clerk :	May I have your confirmation number?
Chae-rim :	Yes, 520-0698.
Reservation clerk :	Okay ma'am, I have your reservation. How would you like to change it?
Chae-rim :	Actually, I've booked a flight 876 going to

	New York. But I want to take a morning flight, if possible.
Reservation clerk :	All right, ma'am. Just a moment. We have a flight departing at 6:30 am. Would you like that?
Chae-rim :	Yes, I'd like to take that. Is there any charges for this?
Reservation clerk :	No. It's free of charge, ma'am.
Chae-rim :	That's nice. Thank you so much.
Reservation clerk :	You're welcome. Have a great day!

Special request

CD TRACK 3

Reservation clerk :	Good afternoon, Thank you for calling Smile Airlines reservation. This is Miss Kim speaking. How can I help you?
Andy :	I have a question for you. I'm going to Seattle on Apr. 8, and I want to request special meals for my family. Is it possible?
Reservation clerk :	Certainly, may I have your confirmation number?

Andy : Yes, 520-0698.

Reservation clerk : Okay, sir. What kind of meal would you like to have?

Andy : I want to have a vegetarian meal, and a kids meal for my daughter, please.

Reservation clerk : Sure, one moment please... you're all set. Vegetarian and kids meals will be served during your flight.

Andy : By the way, what time should I arrive at the airport for check-in?

Reservation clerk : We recommend you to arrive at the airport at least two hours prior to the departure time. Is there anything else I can help you with, sir?

Andy : No. That's all, thank you!

Reservation clerk : Thank you!

Cancellation CD TRACK 4

Reservation clerk : Good afternoon, Smile Airlines. How can I help you?

Bruce: Hi, I would like to cancel my flight reservation. Could you please check and see if there is any cancellation fee.

Reservation clerk: Of course, sir. Can I have your name?

Bruce: Bruce Kwon, Kwon is my last name and **I'm supposed to** fly on the 21st of May.

Reservation clerk: **Could you spell your last name,** sir?

Bruce: K-W-O-N, Kwon.

Reservation clerk: Thank you, just one moment, sir. Alright, Your reservation has just been cancelled without any charges. Is there anything else I can do for you, sir?

Bruce: No, that will be all. Thank you very much.

Reservation clerk: Thank you. Have a nice day.

Ticketing

CD TRACK 5

Reservation agent: Good afternoon, sir. How may I help you?

Dong-gun: I need to purchase a round-trip ticket to Los Angeles.

Reservation agent: **Do you have a reservation?**

Dong-gun :	Yes, I do. My name is Dong-gun Jang and I was booked on Flight 799 going to L.A. next Tuesday at 3 pm.
Reservation agent :	Yes, sir. **Would you like to pay in cash or by credit card?**
Dong-gun :	Well, **how much does it cost?**
Reservation agent :	OOH... I'm so sorry. That will be 1,568,000 won.
Dong-gun :	Okay, I'm going to pay with Visa.
Reservation agent :	Thank you, sir. You may get your ticket here or by email. If you receive an e-ticket, just print it out and bring it to the airport.
Dong-gun :	That sounds great. I prefer to have it by email. Please send it to dglove@hotmail.com.
Reservation agent :	dglove@hotmail.com. Thank you very much, sir. If you don't get it in your email by tomorrow, please let us know and we'll be glad to help you again.
Dong-gun :	OK, thank you.
Reservation agent :	You're welcome. Have a good day.

Grammar point

Be 동사를 사용한 의문문

평서문 주어+be 동사 ~ This is Smile Airlines reservation.

의문문 be 동사+주어 ~ Is this Smile Airlines reservation?

	긍정 대답	부정 대답
Am I...?	Yes, you are.	No, you are not(aren't).
Are you...?	Yes, I am.	No, I am not.
Is she..?	Yes, she is.	No, she is not(isn't).
Is he...?	Yes, he is.	No, he is not(isn't).
Are we...?	Yes, we are.	No, we are not(aren't).
Are you...?	Yes, we are.	No, we are not(aren't).
Are they...?	Yes, they are.	No, they are not(aren't).

일반 동사 의문문

평서문 주어+동사+나머지 부분

의문문 { Do / Does / Did } +주어+동사원형+문장의 나머지 부분

	긍정 대답	부정 대답
Do I like an apple?	Yes, you do.	No, you do not(don't).
you	Yes, I do.	No, I do not(don't).
we	Yes, we do.	No, we do not(don't).
they	Yes, they do.	No, they do not(don't).
Does she like an apple?	Yes, she does.	No, she does(doesn't).
he	Yes, he does.	No, he does(doesn't).
it	Yes, it does.	No, it does(doesn't).

01

I'd like to make a reservation for a flight to New York.

Expression

Is this Smile Airlines reservations?
스마일항공사 예약부인가요?

전화를 받을 때 "저는 Sarah인데요"라는 표현을 영어에서는 "I am Sarah."라고 하지 않고, "This is Sarah."라고 한다. 그럼, Smile항공사 예약부에 전화를 해서 먼저 확인하려고 할 때는 "Is this Smile Airlines reservations?"이라고 물어보면 된다.

How can I help you?
무엇을 도와드릴까요?

상점, 식당, 호텔 등 일상생활에서 흔히 들을 수 있는 표현이다.

What can I do for you?
May(can) I help you?
Is there anything I can do for you?

Language focus

at 9:30 / on Monday / in July, etc.

We often use these prepositions before time/days/months.

	*at*	*7 o'clock* 9:30 *midnight, etc* *night/the end of...*	I wake up *at 7 o'clock*. I start work *at 9:30*.
	*on*	Monday(s), Tuesday(s), etc. July 25th, October 10th, etc. Monday morning, Tuesday afternoon, Saturday night, etc.	

You can say :

See you *on Sunday*. or See you *Sunday*. (with or without **on**)

The concert is *on June 22*. or The concert is *June 22*.

	*in*	April, June, etc. 2009, 1999, etc. the spring/summer/fall/winter the morning/afternoon/evening

- We don't use *at/on/in* before *next/last/this/every*.
- I'm leaving *next Monday* (not on next Monday)
- What are you doing *this weekend*?

01

I'd like to make a reservation for a flight to New York.

Practice

Complete the sentences with at/on/in.

1. I was born .... 1990.
2. The store opens .... 9 o'clock in the morning.
3. I like to look at the stars .... night.
4. My sister is getting married .... June.
5. I'm going to move out .... the end of the month.
6. I don't like to get up early .... the morning.
7. I'll call you .... Tuesday.

Exercise

1. 라스베가스행 왕복 비행기표를 살 수 있을까요?

....

2. 언제 출발하실 계획이십니까?

....

3. 당신의 예약은 추가 수수료 없이 취소되었습니다.

....

4. 일등석을 원하세요, 일반석을 원하세요?

....

5. 항공권은 이메일로 받아보실 것입니다.

....

6. 편도와 왕복 중 어떤 것을 원하세요?

....

7. 여석이 있는지 알아볼게요.

....

8. 비용을 얼마나 지불해야 하죠?

....

Discussion

If you go to Busan from Seoul for a vacation, what kind of transportation do you want to use?

A : Let me think. Umm... I would drive my car since I can make my own schedule.

B : Can you be a little bit more specific?

A : Sure. I can drive when I want, and I can stop if I don't want to drive. I can also have a meal if I am hungry. That's why I would drive. What about you?

B : I would take a plane because it is fast. Even though it is expensive, I can save time and enjoy my vacation.

휴가로 서울에서 부산으로 간다면, 어떤 교통수단을 이용하겠는가?

A : 좀 생각을 해볼게요. 음... 저는 제 차로 가겠어요. 저만의 스케줄을 짤 수 있으니까요.

B : 좀 더 자세하게 얘기해 주시겠어요?

A : 물론이죠. 제가 원할 때 운전하고 원하지 않을 때는 쉴 수 있지요. 배가 고프면 음식을 먹을 수도 있고요. 그래서 저는 제 차를 가지고 가겠어요. 당신은요?

B : 저는 비행기를 타겠어요. 빠르잖아요. 약간 비싸기는 해도, 시간을 아껴서 좀 더 긴 휴가를 즐길 수 있잖아요.

Topics for further discussion

❶ Who would you like to go on vacation with?

❷ What was your best weekend trip?

❸ Which cities in Korea would you like to visit?

기내 휴대품으로서의 향수도 위험?

향기 나는 향수도 항공에서는 위험품으로 취급한다. 그 이유는 향수가 휘발성을 갖고 있어 폭발의 위험이 있기 때문이다. 그렇다고 아예 못가지고 가는 것은 아니다. 휴대하고 탈 수 있지만 양으로 제한을 받는다. 향수나 헤어스프레이, 에어로졸 등은 용기당 1.5kg 또는 1.5ℓ 이내로 1인당 총 2kg이나 2ℓ 까지만 기내반입이 허용된다. 여행용으로 평소에 사용하던 향수를 가지고 가는 정도로는 무난한 양이니 크게 걱정할 바는 못된다.

기내에서 판매하는 향수를 살펴보면 모두 용량이 최대 100㎖ 미만인 것을 볼 수 있다. 하지만 이 향수나 헤어스프레이, 에어로졸이 소량으로 기내 휴대는 가능하지만 가방에 넣어 화물칸에 싣지는 못한다. 화물칸에는 에어컨 시설이 없기 때문에 높은 고도와 온도에 폭발의 위험요소가 될 수 있기 때문이다.

한편 건전지도 기내 휴대제한 품목 중 하나이다. 하지만 요즘 워크맨 등 휴대용 카세트가 보편화되면서 이들 카세트에 사용되는 건전지는 카세트에 내장된 상태로는 반입이 허용되며, 추가로 가지고 가는 건전지는 객실 승무원들이 별도로 보관했다가 도착지에서 전달하도록 하고 있다.

유나이티드항공 *United Airlines*

1930년 세계 최초로 객실 승무원 제도를 도입한 미국 유나이티드항공사의 Easy Check-in System. Easy Check-in은 항공사 직원의 도움 없이 승객이 직접 체크인 할 수 있는 새로운 서비스이다.

Unit 02

Do you have any rooms available?

02 *Do you have any rooms available?*

Before we go

- Where is the best place you have ever stayed at during a trip?
- Can you name the most famous hotel in Korea?

Words and phrases

- room reservation
- single(room)/double(room)/twin(room)
- with a view
- rate
- put up
- be filled up
- book
- confirmation number
- expiration date

Room reservation

CD TRACK 1

(Chae-rim is calling the Monte Hotel at New York)

Receptionist : Good afternoon! Reservations Department, this is John Smith speaking, how may I help you?

Chae-rim : Good afternoon! I'd like to make a reservation. **Do you have any rooms available** on June 7th?

Receptionist : Certainly, ma'am. For how many nights are you going to stay, ma'am?

Chae-rim : I am going to stay for four nights.

Receptionist : **What kind of room would you like** to reserve, ma'am?

Chae-rim : A double room, please.

Receptionist : **How many are there in your party?**

Chae-rim : Three, including a baby.

Receptionist : Shall I request a baby crib for your baby, ma'am?

Chae-rim : That will be wonderful!

Receptionist : May I have your name, please?

Chae-rim : Chae-rim Lee.

Receptionist : How do you spell your name?

Chae-rim : C-H-A-E-R-I-M and my last name is Lee, L-E-E.

Receptionist : Thank you, Ms. Lee. May I have your card number and expiration date, please?

Chae-rim : Sure. It's VISA and the number is 4105 2482 3199 7014, and the expiration date is 10/20.

Receptionist : Let me repeat your card number 4105 2482 3199 7014 and the expiration date is October 20th. Is that right?

Chae-rim : Yes it is.

Receptionist : **May I have your contact number**, Ms. Lee?

Chae-rim : It is 520-0710.

Receptionist : Let me confirm your reservation. You are booked in a double room for 4 nights from June. 7th to June. 11th. Your confirmation number is K235J. The room rate is $199 +10% tax per night. When we check you in, we'll need your picture ID and the credit card that you made the reservation with. Anything else,

	Ms. Lee?
Chae-rim :	No, that's all.
Receptionist :	Thank you very much. We look forward to seeing you on June 7th and thanks for calling Monte Hotel.

Changing a reservation

CD TRACK 2

Reservation clerk :	Hello. This is Hilton Hotel reservations. How can I help you?
Chae-rim :	Yes, I have a reservation from the 18th to the 23rd of July for a single non-smoking room with a shower and balcony.
Reservation clerk :	May I have your name, please?
Chae-rim :	Chae-rim Lee.
Reservation clerk :	Could you spell it for me, please?
Chae-rim :	C-H-A-E-R-I-M. I would like to change the date, if possible, from 20th to the 24th of July.
Reservation clerk :	Could you please hold. Let me see... I think it's going to be no problem. From 20th to

	the 24th, you said?
Chae-rim :	Yes, that's right.
Reservation clerk :	I'm just checking... the 20th to the 24th... Yes, that's fine, Ms. Lee, a single nonsmoking room with a shower and balcony for 4 nights.
Chae-rim :	Thank you, so that's fixed up then?
Reservation clerk :	Yes, It's done, Ms. Lee. We look forward to welcoming you on the 20th.
Chae-rim :	Thank you. Bye.
Reservation clerk :	Good bye.

Grammar point

조동사를 사용한 의문문

평서문 주어+조동사+동사+문장 나머지 — I may see your ticket.

의문문 조동사+주어+동사+문장 나머지 — May I see your ticket?

• Will(be going to) : ~할 것이다.	• Will you come tomorrow?
• Can(be able to) : ~할 수 있다.	• Can you play the piano?
• May ~일지도 모른다 : ~해도 된다.	• May I use your pencil?
• Must(have to) : ~해야만 한다.	• Do I have to finish it now?
• Should(ought to) : ~해야 한다. ~임에 틀림없다.	• You should do it now.
• Had better : ~하는 게 낫겠다.	• We had better leave now.

	긍정 대답	부정 대답
Can I ~?	Yes, you can.	No, you cannot(can't).
Can you ~?	Yes, I can.	No, I cannot(can't).
Can she ~?	Yes, she can.	No, she cannot(can't).
Can he ~?	Yes, he can.	No, he cannot(can't).
Can it ~?	Yes, it can.	No, it cannot(can't).
Can they ~?	Yes, they can.	No, they cannot(can't).

Expression

Do you have a room available

빈 방 있나요?

'Available'의 사전적 의미는 '이용 가능한'이라는 뜻이다. 그래서 "시간 있나요?"라고 물어볼 때도 "Do you have time available?"이라고 표현할 수 있다. "빈 방 있나요?"라는 의미로 "Do you have a vacancy?"라는 표현도 흔히 쓴다.

What's the rate?

가격은 어떻게 되나요?

숙박 비용을 물을 때 '요금, 가격'이라는 뜻을 가진 'rate'를 써서 "what's the rate?"라고 물어본다. 또한 교통 요금을 묻는 표현으로는 "What's the fare?"가 있다. 'fare'는 '승차 운임'을 뜻한다. 'a taxi/bus/train fare' 등으로 표현하여 '택시/버스/기차 요금'을 말할 수 있다. "What's the price?"라고 물을 때 'price'는 '팔리는 물건 등의 가격'을 일컫는 말이다.

Language focus

in, at, and on(places 1)

in

in a room
in a store
in a car
in the water

in a yard
in a town
in a park
in Korea

- "Where's John?" "*In the kitchen/In the back yard/In Seoul*"
- What's *in that box/in that bag/in that closet*?
- She works *in a store/in a bank/in a factory*.

at

at the bus stop

at the door

at the traffic light

at her desk

- There's a man *at the bus stop/at the door*.
- The car is waiting *at the traffic light*.
- She is working *at her desk*.

on

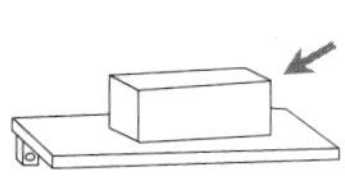

on a shelf
on a plate
on a balcony
on the floor, etc.

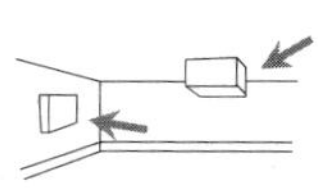

on a wall
on the ceiling
on a door, etc.

- There are some books *on the shelf* and some pictures *on the wall*.
- Don't sit *on the grass*.
- There's a stamp *on the envelope*.

Practice

Complete the sentences with in/at/on.

1. What do you have .... the bag?
2. There are a lot of fish .... this river.
3. There's a man .... the roof. What is he doing?
4. There's a gas station .... the end of the block.
5. There's a mirror .... the wall .... the living room.
6. I looked at the list of names. My name was .... the bottom of the list.
7. "Is the post office near here?" "Yes, turn left .... the traffic light."
8. It's difficult to carry a lot of things .... a bicycle.
9. I have a friend living .... Toronto.
10. I think I heard the doorbell. There's somebody .... the door.

Exercise

1. 객실 예약부입니다. 무엇을 도와드릴까요?

....

2. 빈 방 있나요?

....

3. 어떤 방을 원하세요?

....

4. 이틀 동안 머물 욕실 딸린 1인용 방이요.

....

5. 호수가 잘 내려다보이는 방 하나 있습니다. 성함이 어떻게 되세요?

....

6. 박은세라고 합니다. 박이 성이예요.

....

Discussion

What do you think of staying at a five star hotel during a trip?

A : What do you think of staying at a five star hotel during a trip?

B : I think sleeping soundly is the most important thing when traveling.

A : **Why do you think so?**

B : If you can't sleep well and feel tired all day long, you can't enjoy your trip at all. So, I think staying at a good hotel is necessary.

A : **That makes sense.** But traveling is expensive. So, I would rather save money by staying at a cheap place.

여행기간 동안 특급 호텔에 머무르는 것에 대해 어떻게 생각하세요?

A : 여행기간 동안 비싼 호텔에 머무르는 것에 대해 어떻게 생각하세요?

B : 저는 여행할 때 편히 잠자는 것이 가장 중요하다고 생각합니다.

A : **왜 그렇게 생각하세요?**

B : 만약 잠을 잘 자지 못한다면 하루 종일 피곤할 것이고, 결국 여행을 즐길 수 없게 되죠. 그래서 저는 좋은 호텔에 머무르는 것이 필요하다고 생각해요.

A : **이해가 되네요.** 그렇지만 여행에는 많은 돈이 들지요. 그래서 전 싼 호텔에 머무르면서 여행비용을 줄이겠어요.

Tip

What do you think of ~대해 논의해 봅시다.

토론을 시작할 때 쓸 수 있는 표현이다.

- Let's talk about~ ~에 관해 얘기해 봅시다.
- Let's discuss about~ ~에 대해 토론해 봅시다.
- Express/tell your idea freely. 서슴지 말고 의견을 말씀해 주세요.
- Can I ask your opinion on this subject? 이 주제에 관해 의견을 여쭤 봐도 될까요?

Why do you think so? 왜 그렇게 생각하세요?

토론에서 가장 중요한 것은 자신의 의견을 말하는 것과 거기에 맞는 정당한 이유를 설명하는 것이다. 상대방의 의견에 "Why do you think so?"라고 계속적으로 묻고, 또한 자신의 의견을 피력할 때도 언제나 충분한 의견을 제시하는 것이 토론의 기본이다.

That makes sense. 이해가 돼.

토론시 자신의 의견만을 고집하기보다는 상대방이 설득력 있게 말할 때, 상대방의 의견을 존중해 주는 것도 좋은 토론 습관이다. 상대방의 의견이 이치에 맞는다고 생각할 때 쓸 수 있는 표현이 "That makes sense."이다.

- I see your point. 무슨 말인지 알 것 같네요.
- It may be true. 그럴 수도 있겠네요.

Topics for further discussion

❶ When you travel, do you prefer staying at expensive hotels or budget hotels?

❷ What skills do people need to learn if they want to work at a hotel?

❸ What qualities distinguish good hotels from average hotels?

Reading

Hidden Amenities at Incheon International Airport

Every day Incheon International Airport handles about 80,000 passengers, 600 arriving and departing flights, 7,000 tons of cargo, and more than 30,000 staff who work around the clock – it is like a small city, as claimed in the soap opera "Air City." The drama features incidents at Incheon International Airport, thus revealing every corner of the huge facility which ordinary passengers never see.

Some of the areas of the airport that are used in the soap opera are staff-only zones and others are tucked-away areas that most travelers have not been informed about.

For a short rest

After enjoying shopping at duty free shops, passengers get tired even before starting their trip – the airport stretches 1 kilometer from east to west. First class passengers are not the only ones who can use lounges: communications companies provide resting places for their members. Those with SK Telecom's Leaders' Club card, TTL VIP or ting VIP cards, or KTF's membership cards can relax at the company lounges located on the fourth floor as well as enjoy snacks and drinks. Internet access and magazines are also available.

For a long rest

Your plane is delayed or you have a lengthy stopover time, and you need sleep.

The transit hotel "Air Garden" is on the fourth floor. The majority of the guests are Russians who arrive from the U.S. and are catching a connecting flight to Russia the following morning, according to a staff member of the Sheraton Grande Walkerhill, operator of Air Garden. The hotel rate is 45,000 won excluding tax for six hours.

If you don't want to pay for a rest, you can use chairs in the terminal.

If you are searching for a quiet place to sleep, go to the fourth floor where few passengers visit. Passengers can also take a long rest at prayer rooms equipped with chairs and floor cushions. A sign there says, "You cannot use this room for a purpose other than religious activity." Well, people sometimes fall asleep during prayer.

For washing and relaxation

A sauna on the first basement is available 24 hours. The price is 10,000 won during daytime and 15,000 won at night including a sleeping room. Visitors can also get a haircut and have their shoes shined.

You can also use a shower room at a massage center on the fourth floor for 8,000 won per 30 minutes. The center provides a 70-minute aroma massage for 120,000 won and a 50-minute body and foot massage for 60,000 won.

The majority of customers at the hair salon on the first basement level are newlyweds who come to the airport immediately after their wedding. There you can have your hair trimmed for around 30,000 won.

Other amenities

A nursery equipped with toys and a television is located near Gate 29.

Passengers can deposit their belongings in a locker near the nursery after obtaining locker keys using ID cards as a deposit.

There is a medical center on the first basement level. It provides treatment as well as consultation about foreign diseases and it opened a jetlag clinic last year.

(based on, Sept. 15. 2009)

그랜드하얏트호텔*Grand Hyatt Hotel*

호텔의 최고급 이미지를 전달하기 위한 광고는 특급 호텔의 주요 광고 전략이다.

Unit 03

May I see your ticket and passport?

03 May I see your ticket and passport?

Before we go

- Have you ever flown on a plane? How did it feel the first time you flew?
- How often do you travel by plane?
- What's your favorite country? Why?

Words and phrases

- rack/compartment/overhead bin
- check-in counter
- window seat/aisle seat
- fasten seatbelt
- baggage/carry-on baggage/checked baggage
- boarding pass
- passport

Check-in CD TRACK 1

Chae-rim : Excuse me. **Is this the check-in counter** for Smile Airlines?

Airline staff : Yes, ma'am.

Chae-rim : I'd like to check-in, please.

Airline staff : **May I see your ticket and passport,** please?

Chae-rim : **Here you are.**

Airline staff : Are you going to New York on Flight 124?

Chae-rim : Yes.

Airline staff : **Would you like a window seat or an aisle seat?**

Chae-rim : I'd like a window seat.

Airline staff : **Do you have any baggage to check?**

Chae-rim : Just one. I will take this bag as carry-on luggage.

Airline staff : Are there lighters, sprays, knives or any breakable things in your luggage?

Chae-rim : No.

Airline staff : Would you please put your baggage on the scale?

Chae-rim : Sure.

Airline staff : All right. Here are your boarding pass, baggage claim ticket and passport. You'll be boarding at Gate 56 and your seat is 21A window. Please be sure to be on time. Have a nice flight.

Chae-rim : Thank you very much. Where can I pick duty-free items up?

Airline staff : You can pick them up past the security check-in.

Finding a seat

CD TRACK 2

Flight attendant : Welcome on board.

Chae-rim : **Can you tell me where my seat is?**

Flight attendant : Let me see your boarding pass, please.

Chae-rim : Here it is.

Flight attendant : 21A. Right here, ma'am.

Chae-rim : Thank you. **Where can I put my bag?**

Flight attendant : You can put it on the rack over your head or underneath the seat in front of you. Let

	me help you.
Chae-rim :	Thank you so much. I appreciate it.
Flight attendant :	Not at all.

Fastening a seatbelt

CD TRACK 3

Flight attendant :	**Could you please fasten your seatbelt?** We will be taking off shortly.
Chae-rim :	**I beg your pardon?**
Flight attendant :	Fasten your seat belt, please.
Chae-rim :	I am sorry, but can you show me how to fasten the seatbelt?
Flight attendant :	Certainly, ma'am. Pull in this way and insert this part into the buckle.
Chae-rim :	Oh, I see. Thanks a lot.
Flight attendant :	You're welcome.
Chae-rim :	Can I have a pillow and blanket, please?
Flight attendant :	Sure. I'll be right back.

Grammar point

의문사를 사용한 의문문(1)

Where is Gate 9?

의문사 who(누가)/whom(누구를)/whose(누구의)/what(무엇이)/which(어떤 것이)/when(언제)/where(어디서)/why(왜)/how(어떻게)

의문사	+	be 동사	+	주어	+	문장 나머지
Who		am		I?		
Who		are		you?		
Who		is		he?		
Who		is		she?		
Who		are		they?		
What		is		it?		
What		are		they?		

의문사를 사용한 의문문(2)

Where can I put my bag?

의문사	+	조동사	+	주어	+	동사+문장 나머지
Where		can		I		put the bag?
Where				you		
Where				he		
Where				she		
Where				it		
Where				they		
Where				we		

Expression

Here you are. 여기 있어요.

물건을 건네주면서 쓸 수 있는 표현이다. 식사 도중에 누군가가 "Could you pass me the salt, please?"라고 묻는다면 "Here you are." 라고 말할 수 있다.

Here it is. 여기 있어요.　　Here we go. 여기요.

Let me+동사원형 ~시켜 달라, ~해보고 싶다.

가벼운 제안이나 요구의 의미로 쓸 수 있다. "제가 이야기 하나 해 드릴게요"라고 말할 때 "Let me tell you something."이라고 표현할 수 있다. 우리가 흔히 자신을 소개할 때 "Let me introduce myself."라고 하는데 이도 'Let me+동사'의 동일한 쓰임이다.

I beg your pardon(↗)? 네? 뭐라고 하셨나요?

"I beg your pardon(↘)"이라고 억양을 내리면 "Excuse me."와 동일한 표현으로 '실례합니다'의 뜻이지만, 억양을 올려서 얘기하면 '뭐라고 하셨나요?'의 뜻이 된다.

Beg your pardon?　　Pardon (me)?

I'm sorry?　　Can you say that again, please?

Language focus

in, at, and on(Places 2)

in

in bed	*in* the hospital	*in* the sky
in the world	*in* a newspaper/*in* a book	*in* a photograph/*in* a picture
in a car/in a taxi	*in* the middle	

"Where's Kelly?" "she's *in* **bed.**" My sister is sick. She is *in* **the hospital.**
I like to look at the stars *in* **the sky at night.**

at

at work *at* the station/*at* the airport
at the post office/*at* the supermarket
at Tom's(house)/*at* the doctor's(office)/at the hairdresser's, etc.
at a concert/at a party/*at* a football game, etc.

"Where's Kelly?" "She's *at* **work.**"
I'll see you *at* **the airport.** I saw Tim *at* **the doctor's office.**

- You can say **be/stay** *at* **home** or **be/stay home**(with or without **at**)
- You can often use in or *at* for **hotels** and **restaurants.**
- you can say *in* **school** or *at* **school**, but there is a difference.
  She's **at** school means she is there now.
  She's **in** school means she is a student.

on

on a bus/*on* a train/*on* a plane etc.
on a the first floor/*on* the second floor etc.
on a street
on the way(to...)/*on* the way home

The office is *on* **the first floor.** My brother lives *on* **a nice street.**
I met Kim *on* **the way** to work/*on* **my way** home.

Practice

Complete the sentences with in/at/on.

1. There is a big table .... the middle of the room.
2. What is the longest river .... the world?
3. Were there many people .... the concert last night?
4. I'm going to meet her .... the station.
5. I don't believe everything you see .... the newspaper.
6. I met Anne .... my way home.

Exercise

1. 영국행 비행기 체크인 데스크가 여기 맞나요?

   ....

2. 네. 비행기 티켓과 여권 보여주세요.

   ....

3. 여기 있습니다.

   ....

4. 창 쪽 좌석과 통로 좌석 중 어느 것을 원하세요?

   ....

5. 몇 번 게이트에서 비행기를 타야 하나요?

   ....

6. 어느 곳에 짐을 놓을까요?

   ....

7. 안전벨트를 어떻게 착용하는지 알려주시겠어요?

   ....

Discussion

Which do you prefer, a window seat or an aisle seat?

A : Which do you prefer, a window seat or an aisle seat?

B : I prefer a window seat to an aisle seat.

A : **How come?**

B : I can see the outside. I can look down on the whole city of Seoul from the sky. It's exciting.

A : **What you are saying is true to some extent,** I think. But a window seat is still inconvenient.

B : **What do you mean** by 'inconvenient'?

A : When you go to the lavatory, you have to disturb the person sitting on the aisle seat.

창 쪽 좌석과 통로 좌석

A : 창 쪽 조석과 통로 좌석 중 어느 것을 선호하세요?

B : 저는 통로 좌석보다는 창 쪽 좌석이 좋아요.

A : **왜요?**

B : 밖을 볼 수 있잖아요. 하늘에서 서울시 전체를 내려다볼 수 있어 신나잖아요.

A : **말씀하시는 게 어느 부분은 맞는 말입니다만,** 저는 창 쪽 좌석은 약간 불편한 것 같아요.

B : 불편하다니 **무슨 말씀이세요?**

A : 화장실을 가려고 할 때 통로 좌석에 앉은 사람에게 양해를 구해야 하잖아요.

Tip

What you are saying is true to some extent. 말씀하시는 게 어느 정도는 맞습니다.

상대 토론자의 의견에 어느 정도 수긍할 때 쓰는 표현이다. "What you are saying is true to some extent." 다음에 '그러나'라는 접속사 'but'을 붙여서 반대의 의견을 말할 수도 있다.

- I can agree some parts of your opinion.
- What you are saying can be true.

What do you mean~? 무슨 의미인가요?

토론에서 상대방의 의견을 잘 이해하지 못했을 때 쓰는 표현이다.

- I don't get it. 잘 모르겠어요.
- What does that mean? 그게 무슨 말씀이세요?
- Can you be more specific? 좀 더 상세히 설명해 주시겠어요?
- I didn't understand what you are saying. 무슨 말씀인지 모르겠어요.

Topics for further discussion

❶ What would you do if a little girl behind you kept kicking the seat?

❷ Have you ever bought a business or first class airline ticket?

❸ Why do you think people pay more to fly first class?

Reading

Korean Air, Asiana Airlines steps up online ticket sales

In August this year through its Internet sales outlets, the online air ticket sales in August broke down to 8,487 million won in domestic air tickets and 2,816 million won in international air tickets, according to Korean Air.

It was the first time that online monthly air ticket sales figures surpassed the 10 billion won mark since Internet air ticket sales came into service. Online air ticket sales increased by 113 percent from the same period a year earlier.

One major factor behind the explosive buying demand for online air ticket sales is that online air ticket buying is much easier and cheaper than off-line air ticketing and reservations.

According to KAL figures, online sales of domestic air tickets against total air ticket sales take 12 percent while online international air ticket sales account for 1.6 percent of the total sales. The Internet air ticket sales are increasing steadily against the backdrop of ever-increasing number of Internet users in Korea.

Asiana Airlines, in the meantime, saw its air ticket sales through Internet sales outlets increase to 5 billion won in August this year, up

2 billion from 3 billion won registered a year earlier.

Encouraged by the trend, Asiana Airlines plans to increase its online air ticket sales next year up to 55 billion won in domestic line sales and 6 billion won in international air tickets.

The ratio of online air ticket sales against the total air ticket sales for Asiana Airlines is 12.1 percent for domestic air tickets and 1.3 percent for international air tickets, almost the same as that of Korean Air.

Unlike offline air ticket sales, air carriers can reduce sales costs by using Internet sales outlets effectively. Air ticket sale commissions, which would otherwise be paid to sales agents, can be saved, not to mention reduced consulting staff member labor costs.

Thanks to the development of Internet air ticket and reservation technology, cyber marketing is expected to play a more important role for air carriers in boosting air ticket sales in the years to come.

(source from travelinfo.co.kr)

Exit row seat : 비상구 좌석

출입문 쪽 앞의 넓은 자리는 일명 '비상구 좌석'이라 하는데 이 좌석은 여유가 없는 기내 좌석 중 비교적 앞이 트여 있어 손님들이 많이 선호한다. 하지만 단순히 앞자리, 넓은 자리가 아닌 '비상구 좌석'이라 이름 붙여진 내부적 의미는 '승객이 기내 통로를 이용하지 않고 어떠한 기내 구조물의 방해 없이 바로 비상구에 접근할 수 있는 좌석으로 이곳을 지나지 않고서는 비상구에 접근하지 못하는 좌석'이란 뜻이다.

비상구 좌석 배정의 최우선 순위는 탑승 승무원이나 추가 탑승 승무원이고 그 다음이 항공사 직원이다. 승무원이나 항공사 직원 탑승객이 없을 경우 비상시 승무원의 지시에 따라 비상구를 작동, 다른 승객들의 탈출을 도울 수 있는 신체 건강한 승객으로 승무원을 도와 협력할 의사가 있는 사람이어야 한다.

하지만 15세 미만으로 오히려 성인의 도움이 필요한 어린이 승객이나 이런 어린이를 동반한 승객, 신체적으로 근력과 유연성이 부족해 상하좌우로 잡고 당기거나 밀어서 비상구를 여는 동작, 비상문을 옮기는 동작, 비상구 주변 장애물을 제거하는 동작, 팽창된 슬라이드의 균형을 잡는 동작, 비상사태 시 즉각 탈출해 슬라이드로 내려오는 승객들을 일으켜 세우는 동작 등을 수행하기 어려운 승객은 비상구 좌석에 앉지 못하게 되어 있다.

또한 안전규칙의 내용을 이해하지 못하거나 한국어 또는 영어를 이해하지 못하는 승객, 청력·시력·언어 장애가 있는 승객, 승무원을 도와 다른 승객의 탈출을 돕는다는 비상구 좌석의 착석 규정을 준수할 의사가 없는 승객 등은 본인이 원해도 그 좌석에는 앉을 수 없는 것이다.

그러므로 비상구 좌석을 배정하기 위해서는 탑승수속 카운터에서 체크인을 진행하는 직원이 승객의 적합 여부를 확인하고, 비상구 좌석 안내 및 비상시 협력 의사를 타진해 승객이 승낙하는 경우에 탑승권을 발급하게 된다.

Aircraft Type
B 747-400 / 300 (version 7441/ 7431)

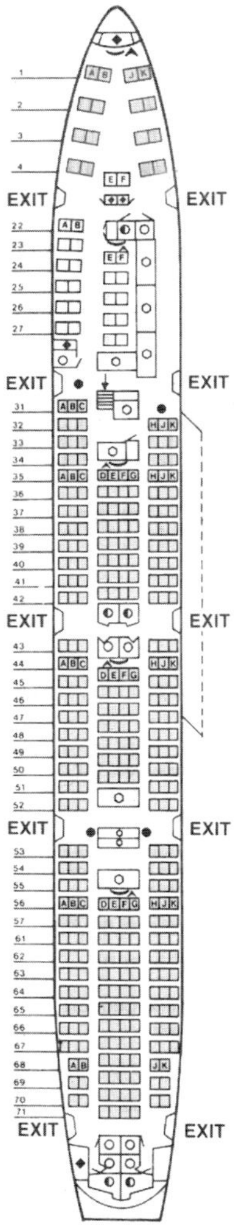

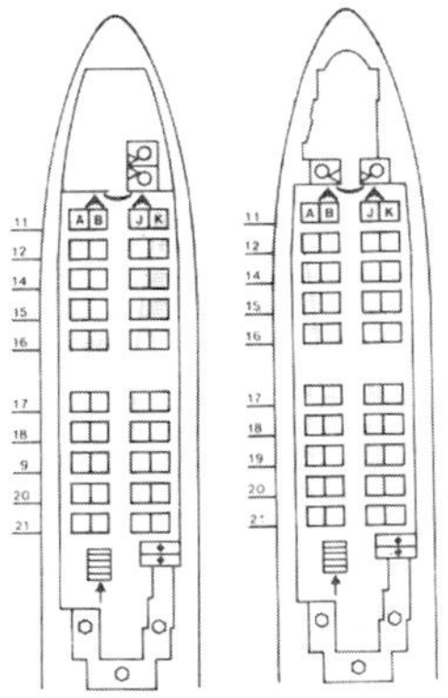

B 747-400 (version 7441)

B 747-300 (version 7431)

Upper deck

Aircraft Type Code 744/743

Seat plan

Royal First Class Row 1-4	18 seats
Royal Executive Class Upper deck Row 11-21	40 seats
Royal Executive Class Main deck Row 22-27	22 seats
Economy Row 31-71	325 seats

Facility and Comfort

- ◆ Coat room
- ○ Toilette
- ◐ Toilette with diaper change board
- ○ Galley
- ^ Baby bassinets
- ‿ Video screen
- ● Video monitor

Carry - on bagage and Safety

Carry-on baggage to be placed in overhead locker or under the seat in front only

보잉 747–400 기종의 일반적인 좌석 배치*Seat Map*

03

May I see your ticket and passport?

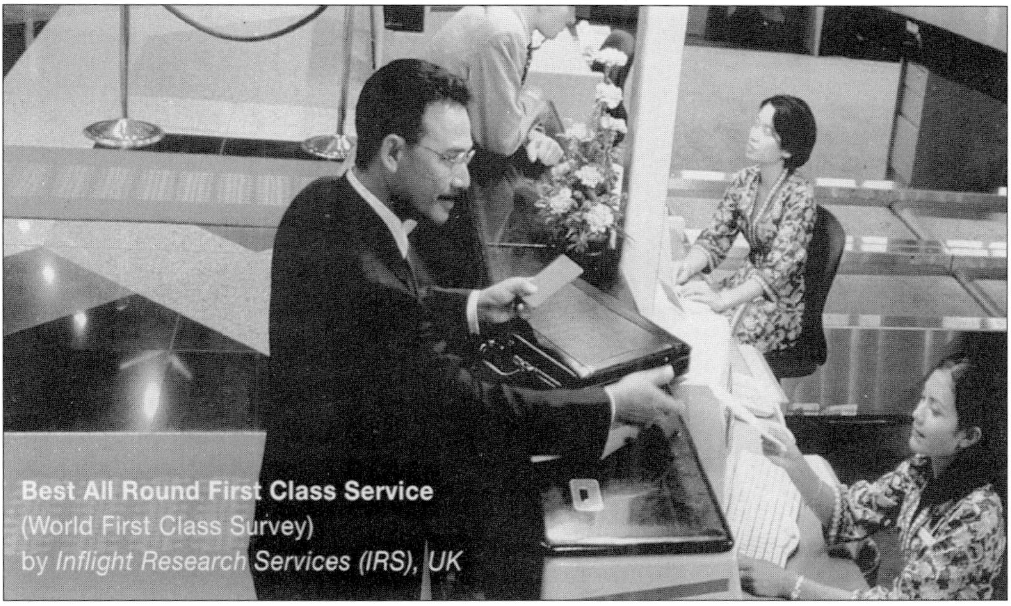

말레이시아항공 *Malaysia Airlines*

영국 IRS(Inflight research services)에서 수여한 최고의 1등석 서비스 제공 항공사에 선정된 바 있는 말레이시아항공은 서비스뿐만 아니라 안전제일 항공사의 이미지를 구축하기 위한 노력을 계속하고 있다.

Unit 04

What would you like to have for dinner?

04 What would you like to have for dinner?

Before we go

- What is the best food you've ever had on a plane?
- Do you have any food you want to try on a plane?
- Have you ever bought something on an airplane?
- What do you want to buy at a duty-free shop?

Words and phrases

- serve
- tray table
- would you mind ~ing
- would you care for
- duty-free
- allowance
- cart
- traveler's check
- endorse
- in-fight magazine

Meal service (1) CD TRACK 1

Flight attendant :	We are serving dinner now. **Which would you like to have for dinner,** beef or fish?
Chae-rim :	What does the beef come with? Could you be a little bit more specific?
Flight attendant :	Grilled beef comes with fried rice, and salmon is served with vegetables.
Chae-rim :	I'll have fish, then.
Flight attendant :	**Would you mind opening** your tray table, please?
Chae-rim :	Of course not.
Flight attendant :	Here you go, and **would you like something to drink?** We have coke, sprite, juice and iced tea.
Chae-rim :	Do you have apple juice?
Flight attendant :	Yes, we do. Here it is, ma'am. Enjoy your meal.
Chae-rim :	Thank you.

Meal service (2) CD TRACK 2

Flight attendant :	Beef or fish, sir?
Andy :	I requested a vegetarian meal when I made the reservation.
Flight attendant :	I'm sorry, sir. May I have your name, please?
Andy :	Yes, I'm Andy Cho.
Flight attendant :	Thank you, I'll check on your meal immediately. (Flight attendant brings the special meal) Here is your meal and we are very sorry to have kept you waiting so long.
Andy :	That's alright and thank you for your help.
Flight attendant :	You're welcome.

Meal service (3) CD TRACK 3

Flight attendant :	What would you like, sir?
Kim :	Well, I'm not hungry. Can I have my meal later, and just a beer for now?

Flight attendant : Of course, sir. Here we go, and just let me know whenever you want your meal.

Kim : Thank you. It's very kind of you.

Flight attendant : Thank you.

In-flight music

CD TRACK 4

Chae-rim : **What kind of music** do you have?

Flight attendant : We have pop, rock, jazz and classical music. You can find our music program in your in-flight magazine.

Chae-rim : Thank you.

(Chae-rim finds out that her headset does not work)

Chae-rim : Excuse me. This headset is not working properly.

Flight attendant : Let me check. (After checking the earphone set for a while) Can you hear it now?

Chae-rim : Yes, it's better now. Thank you.

Flight attendant : My pleasure.

In-flight movie CD TRACK 5

Chae-rim : **What kind of** movie are you showing today?

Flight attendant : It's a comedy. There is information about today's movie in the back.

Chae-rim : Thank you. **When are you going to show it?**

Flight attendant : We will show the movie after the meal, in about 2 and a half hours.

Chae-rim : Thanks. But I can't see the movie screen from this seat. **Can I change my seat?**

Flight attendant : Let me check if there is any empty seat for you. Would you please wait a moment?

Chae-rim : Certainly. Thank you.

In-flight purchase CD TRACK 6

(The duty free cart is passing by Chae-rim's seat)

Flight attendant : Would you like to buy any duty-free items, ma'am?

Chae-rim : Yes, please. What kind of perfume do you

have?

Flight attendant : We have several as you see on the duty-free sales guide.

Chae-rim : I want to get one Chanel No. 5, please. Do you know the allowance of perfumes I can take into New York?

Flight attendant : You may take in 60ml of perfume.

Chae-rim : Okay, how much is it?

Flight attendant : It's 35 US dollars.

Chae-rim : **Do you accept** traveler's checks?

Flight attendant : Certainly, ma'am. Just endorse the check and write your name, passport number and nationality on the back.

Chae-rim : All right. Here you are.

Flight attendant : Thank you. One second, please. **I'll be back** with your change.

Grammar point

선택의문문

두 개 이상의 선택사항에 대한 의문문이다.
어순은 다음과 같고, 선택사항을 열거한 뒤 마지막 선택사항 앞에 'or'을 붙이면 된다.

의문사 + { 조동사 do / does / did } + 주어 + 동사원형 + 문장의 나머지 부분 +, 선택사항 A or 선택사항 B

의문사 + be 동사 + 주어, 선택사항 A or 선택사항 B

- Which do you want to have, beef or chicken?
- Which is yours, this one or that one?

Expression

Surely. I'll be right back. 곧 가져다 드릴게요.

상대방의 요청에 긍정적 대답으로 쓸 수 있는 표현이다.

Just a moment, please. 잠시만 기다려 주십시오.
Certainly sir/ma'am. 물론입니다.
I'll get it for you right away. 곧 가져다 드릴게요.
It will be ready soon. 곧 준비됩니다.

Would you mind ~ing ~해도 괜찮을까요?

'mind'라는 단어의 사전적 의미는 '~에 신경을 쓰다, 싫어하다'라는 뜻으로 "Would you mind opening a window?"를 직역하면 "창문 여는 것이 싫으세요?"의 뜻이다. 따라서 긍정의 대답에는 'not'을 포함하는 부정형으로 대답한다.

긍정 대답	부정 대답
No, I don't mind. 예, 상관없어요.	I am sorry but~
Not at all. Go right ahead.	
Of course not.	
Certainly not.	

Language focus

Some and Any

Look at the examples and complete the information below with some or any.

She made *some sandwiches*.
Can I have *some water*?
Would you like *some fruit*?

He never eats *any vegetables*.
There isn't *any bread*.
Did you buy *any milk*?

- We use .... in positive sentences and with offers and requests.
- We use .... in negative sentences and most questions.
- We use both .... and .... with plural countable nouns and uncountable nouns.

Practice

Complete the sentences with a/an, some or any.

1. Would you like .... more wine, sir?
2. She doesn't want .... glass of wine.
3. Could I have .... salt, please.
4. Are there .... tables free?
5. We've got .... orange juice but we haven't got .... tomato juice.
6. She doesn't like .... kind of cheese.
7. Could I have .... clean knife, please?
8. Can I have .... fried egg and .... bacon for breakfast?

Exercise

1. 저녁식사로 무엇을 드시겠습니까?

   ....

2. 접이식 테이블을 펴주시겠습니까?

   ....

3. 나중에 식사하고 싶습니다.

   ....

4. 어떤 종류의 영화를 좋아하세요?

   ....

5. 좌석을 바꿔도 될까요?

   ....

6. 여행자 수표 받으시나요?

   ....

Seek & Find

How to solve :

The words in the list at the bottom of the page are hidden within the grid on the next page. The words may be forward, backward, up, down or diagonal. They're always in a straight line and never skip letters. You may use some letters more than once.
Circle the first and last letter of each word within the grid, join them with a straight line and cross it off the word list.

AIRLINE	ALLOWANCE	ALTITUDE
ATTENDANT	BAGGAGE	BOARDING
CABIN	CONFIRMATION	CUSTOM
DEPARTURE	FLIGHT	GATEWAY
IMMIGRATION	ITINERARY	LANDING
PASSENGER	PASSPORT	PILLOW
QUARANTINE	SEATBELT	TRANSPORTATION

F	S	N	B	Y	U	T	L	E	B	T	A	E	S	C
E	G	Y	E	R	E	R	N	I	B	A	C	P	O	D
B	N	A	D	A	G	A	L	L	O	W	A	N	C	E
O	I	I	U	R	A	N	P	I	E	S	F	F	U	I
A	D	R	T	E	G	S	J	O	S	I	W	J	S	R
R	N	L	I	N	G	P	P	P	R	D	T	G	T	C
D	A	I	T	I	A	O	O	M	W	E	N	A	O	V
I	L	N	L	T	B	R	A	K	D	P	A	T	M	M
N	A	E	A	I	T	T	A	F	W	A	D	E	X	C
G	E	N	V	H	I	A	B	U	G	R	N	W	N	D
L	S	X	G	O	D	T	E	J	Q	T	E	A	O	K
T	P	I	N	D	M	I	P	D	S	U	T	Y	E	J
O	L	P	I	L	L	O	W	J	U	R	T	D	P	H
F	P	A	S	S	E	N	G	E	R	E	A	X	G	C
N	O	I	T	A	R	G	I	M	M	I	S	G	R	V

Discussion

Should a female Flight attendant be pretty?

A : Do you think female Flight attendants should be pretty?

B : **Surely not.** As long as they serve the passengers with a smile and are kind, I don't think their appearance is important.

A : **I couldn't agree with you more.** I think they should care more about their physical strength than appearance because they work in the air for so many hours straight.

여승무원들의 외모

A : 여승무원들은 예뻐야 한다고 생각하세요?

B : **물론 아니지요.** 미소와 친절함으로 승객들에게 서비스를 제공한다면, 외모는 중요하지 않다고 봐요.

A : **저도 100% 동의해요.** 저는 여승무원들은 외모보다 신체적 건강에 더 신경을 써야 한다고 봐요. 비행기 내에서 장시간 일을 하니까요.

Tip

Surely not. 물론 아니죠.

강한 부정을 나타낼 때 쓰는 표현이다.

- Certainly not.
- Absolutely not.
- No, not at all.
- Of course not.

I couldn't agree with you more. 당신 의견에 100% 동의해요. 대찬성이예요.

토론을 할 때, 상대방과 자신의 의견이 완전히 일치할 때 쓸 수 있는 표현이다.

- I agree with you completely.
- That's what I am saying.
- You can say that again.
- No doubt about it.
- No question about it.
- Absolutely.
- I am with you.

Topics for further discussion

❶ What are some things that tend to bother you on a plane?

❷ What would you do if a flight attendant spilt coffee on you?

일반석 증후군 예방법

일반석 증후군은 비행기 일반석과 같은 비좁은 좌석에서 움직이지 않고 장시간 앉아 있게 될 경우 다리 정맥에 혈전이 형성되는 것을 유발할 수 있다는 가설에 기초하여 명명되었지만, 항공 여행뿐 아니라 장시간 운전을 하거나 장거리 버스, 기차 여행 등에서도 발생할 수 있다.

항공기를 이용한 여행이 날로 증가하고 이에 대한 관심도 자연히 높아지면서 이와 같은 증상을 '일반석 증후군(Economy Class Syndrome)'이라 불리며 기내에서 쉽게 할 수 있는 예방법은 다음과 같다.

1. 기내는 지상보다 공기가 건조한 편이므로 술보다는 물이나 주스 등을 섭취하는 것이 좋고 피부 미용을 위해 크림 타입의 로션을 충분히 바르는 것이 좋다(커피나 차는 이뇨작용이 있기 때문에 수분 손실을 일으킨다).
2. 운동량이 적은 기내에서는 소화가 잘 되지 않고 기내의 압력 저하로 장내 가스가 팽창하므로 탄산음료를 삼가고 적당한 양을 천천히 섭취한다.
3. 자주 자세를 바꿔주거나 주위 사람에게 피해가 되지 않는 범위에서 자리에 앉아 스트레칭 체조를 하고 매 시간마다 자리에 일어나 복도를 걸으며 근육을 풀어주는 것이 혈액순환에 도움이 된다.
4. 복도 쪽 좌석에 앉는 것이 다리를 펼 수 있는 여유 공간을 만드는 데 도움이 된다.
5. 충분한 수면을 취하며 꽉 조이는 거들이나 무릎 아래까지 오는 스타킹 착용을 피하고 품이 넉넉한 옷을 착용한다.

KLM네덜란드항공*KLM Royal Dutch Airlines*

세계 최초의 민간항공사인 네덜란드항공은 암스테르담을 경유하여 유럽 여러 목적지를 비행함으로써 우리나라 승객들로부터 편리한 항공사라는 이미지를 갖고 있다.

Unit 05

What is the purpose of your visit?

05 What is the purpose of your visit?

Before we go

- What was the most expensive thing you had during a trip?
- Will you carry Korean food with you if you are to travel to a foreign country for several months?

Words and phrases

- nationality
- immigration/immigration form
- quarantine
- customs/customs declaration form
- declare
- purpose of visit
- sightseeing
- citizen/resident/visitor
- fill out
- I'm here to~

Documentation

CD TRACK 1

Chae-rim :	**Do I have to fill out** the immigration form?
Flight attendant :	Are you a transit passenger?
Chae-rim :	No. I will stay in the Unites States for two weeks.
Flight attendant :	Are you a U.S. citizen, Canadian citizen, or U.S. resident?
Chae-rim :	No, I am Korean.
Flight attendant :	Well, then, you have to fill out both the immigration form and customs form. **Do you want me to help you** fill out the forms?
Chae-rim :	No, thank you anyway. But, can you tell me when I can use the rest room?
Flight attendant :	I am afraid you will have to wait until after landing.
Chae-rim :	It's sort of an emergency.
Flight attendant :	I am sorry but we are landing at any moment.

Landing CD TRACK 2

Flight attendant: **We are about to land.** Could you pass me your headset?

Chae-rim: Sure, here it is.

Flight attendant: Did you enjoy your flight?

Chae-rim: **So far so good.**

Flight attendant: I am glad to hear that. We hope to serve you again sometime later.

Entry interview (1) CD TRACK 3

Immigration officer: May I see your passport, please?

Chae-rim: Here you are.

Immigration officer: Your nationality, please?

Chae-rim: Korean.

Immigration officer: **What's the purpose of your visit?**

Chae-rim: For sightseeing

Immigration officer: **How long will you stay?**

Chae-rim: For about two weeks.

Immigration officer: Where will you stay?

Chae-rim: I will stay at the Monte Hotel, New York.

Entry interview (2) CD TRACK 4

Chae-rim: Hi, How are you. Here are my passport and the form.

Immigration officer: Business or pleasure?

Chae-rim: **I'm here to** attend a meeting.

Immigration officer: Length of stay?

Chae-rim: 10 days.

Immigration officer: Where will you stay?

Chae-rim: I will stay at the Monte Hotel, New York. Then, I'll visit and stay at my friend's place for 3 days.

Immigration officer: OK. Here is your passport back. Welcome to the United States.

Chae-rim: Thank you.

Entry interview (3) CD TRACK 5

Immigration officer: What's the purpose of your trip?

Chae-rim: I'm here to study at UNLV.

Immigration officer: Are you? What are you going to study?

Chae-rim: I'm majoring in Tourism Management.

Immigration officer: Where will you stay?

Chae-rim: At the dorm.

Immigration officer: Alright. Good luck.

Chae-rim: Thank you. Have a nice day.

Customs inspection CD TRACK 6

Customs officer: **Do you have anything to declare?**

Chae-rim: No, nothing.

Customs officer: Will you open your bag?

Chae-rim: Certainly, sir.

Customs officer: What is this?

Chae-rim: This is a gift for my friend.

Customs officer: Do you have your customs declaration form?

Chae-rim: Yes, here it is.

Grammar point

How를 사용한 의문문

의문사 How는 흔히 형용사나 부사와 함께 쓰이고 어순은 다음과 같다.

How+형용사/부사+ { be 동사 / 조동사 } +주어 ~

혹은 How+형용사/부사+ { do / does / did } +주어+동사 ~

- How old are you?
- How often do you go to a movie?
- How tall is she?
- How soon will you get here?
- How well do you play piano?

Expression

What's the purpose of your visit?
방문 목적은 무엇입니까?

방문 목적을 묻는 말로 입국 심사에서 가장 중요한 부분이다. 여행, 공부, 사업, 회의 참석 등 개인마다 이유는 다양할 텐데, 솔직하게 자신의 입국 이유를 밝히면 된다.

I'm here to attend a conference. 회의에 참석하기 위해 왔어요.
I am here on business. 사업차 왔어요.
I came here for sightseeing / I am here to sightsee. 관광하러 왔어요.
I am here to study physics at New York University.
뉴욕대에서 물리학을 공부하러 왔어요.

be about to

'be going to'와 거의 동일한 의미를 가지며 '곧 ~하려 하다, 막 ~하려 하다'의 뜻으로 미래시제를 대신하여 쓸 수 있다.

We are about to land. 곧 착륙할 것이다.
We are about to close. 곧 폐점합니다.

Exercise

1. 입국신고서를 꼭 작성해야만 하나요?

2. 입국신고서와 세관신고서 모두 작성하셔야 합니다.

3. 방문 목적은 무엇인가요?

4. 신고하실 물품이 있나요?

5. 제가 언제 화장실을 가도 될지 말씀해 주시겠어요?

6. 한 3년 정도 머물 계획입니다.

7. 국적이 어디시죠?

Discussion

Smoking is not allowed in the airplane. Do you think this regulation is good or bad?

A : I think this rule is very bad. People sometimes take a plane for over 10 hours. Banning smoking in the airplane can be cruel for a chain smoker.

B : **Are you joking?** Smoking in the airplane can bring a serious problem like fire.

A : **I don't think so.** Most airplanes have safety precautions for that problem.

B : You have to think about other nonsmoking passengers. Everybody knows that second hand smoke is harmful.

A : **You've got a good point.** But it would not be any trouble to other passengers if we smoked only in the lavatory.

비행기에서 흡연은 규제되고 있다. 이 규제는 필요한가?

A : 저는 이 규제가 아주 나쁘다고 생각합니다. 10시간 이상씩 비행기를 타기도 하는데 비행기 안에서 흡연을 규제하는 것은 줄담배를 피는 흡연가에게는 잔인한 것이라고 봅니다.

B : **농담이시죠?** 비행기 내에서 흡연은 화제와 같은 문제를 일으킬 수도 있어요.

A : **저는 그렇게 생각하지 않아요.** 대개 비행기는 안전장치를 갖추고 있다고 봅니다.

B : 다른 비흡연 승객들도 생각해야죠. 간접흡연이 해롭다는 것은 모든 사람이 알고 있잖아요.

A : **좋은 지적입니다.** 그러나 비행기 내 화장실에서만 담배를 핀다면 다른 승객에게 전혀 피해가 되지 않을 거라고 생각해요.

Tip

Are you joking? 농담이시죠?

상대방이 말하는 것이 믿어지지 않을 때 쓰는 표현이다.

- No kidding. 장난이시겠죠.
- Really? 진심이세요?
- No way. 결코 그럴 수 없죠.
- It is hard to believe. 믿기 어려운 걸요.

I don't think so. 저는 그렇게 생각하지 않아요.

- I can't agree with you. 동의할 수 없네요.
- I have a different opinion. 저의 의견은 달라요.

You got the good point. 좋은 지적입니다.

토론에서는 자신의 주장만을 피력하는 것보다 상대의 의견을 존중하면서 자신의 의견을 펴는 것이 필요하다. 타당한 지적에 대해서는 "That's a good point."와 같은 표현으로 상대의 지적을 먼저 수긍하고 그것에 반대되는 자신의 의견을 말하는 것이 좀 더 설득력을 가진다.

Topics for further discussion

❶ What would you take with you if you are to travel for a year?

❷ Why do you think a visitor needs security checks and customs inspection?

❸ What would you do if the alarm went off when you pass through a security check?

05

Reading

US Tourism Offices Rushing to Korea With Visa Waiver Program

Just as Koreans had long waited for the day when they could travel to the U.S. visa-free, so the Californian tourism commission has anxiously looked forward to it as well.

With the ambitious goal to at least triple the number of Korean tourists to California within the next few years, the Californian Tourism Commission celebrated its grand opening of its Korean office on the day that the Visa Wavier Program kicked off, Nov. 17.

During an opening ceremony at the residence of U.S. Ambassador Kathleen Stephens, the ambassador praised the event, hoping California would become one of the most popular vacation destinations of Koreans in the future.

Susan Wilcox, vice president of the California Travel and Tourism Commission, said in support of the visa waiver program that her commission would project to triple the number of Korean tourists to California in the next three years.

Last year, of 806,175 Koreans visited America, while 331,000 people visited California. The number was the fourth largest group of tourists to California, following British, Japanese and German.

The Californian tourism commission is now the eighth American tourism commission now open in Korea. New York City, Dallas, San Francisco, Los Angeles, the State of Texas, Hawaii and Alaska have tourism promotion offices in Korea, and the visa waiver program is expected to encourage other cities and states to open tourism offices here, said Michael Merner, managing director of the commission overseeing Japan and Korea.

The commission has launched a new web site, www.visitcalifornia.co.kr, and visitors to the office in Seoul would have access to brochures and guide books.

It was expected that the tide of Korean tourists would surge with visa-free entry to the United States, and the Korean airline industry reacted quickly.

Korean Air and Asiana increased flights to the United States. However, David Ruch, CEO of United Airways Korea, said with the global financial crisis, he would have to wait and see if the number will actually pick up.

The west coastal state in America has a variety of attractions. Big cities like Los Angeles and San Francisco are on the want-to-visit list. It is also home for iconic places such as Hollywood and Disneyland.

The economy is the largest among 50 states and has a celebrity governor in Arnold Schwarzenegger. The state capital is Sacramento, yet the biggest city is Los Angeles. It is home to many immigrants, many of whom are Korean.

Merner said the state has so much to explore beyond Los Angeles and San Francisco, the two most well-known tourism destinations in California.

He recommended Yosemite National Park, Napa Valley and San Diego as must-see spots.

The Yosemite National Park is a UNESCO World Heritage site, renowned for granite cliffs, waterfalls, Giant Sequoia groves and other sites. Napa Valley, located just outside of San Francisco, is an emerging name for its wine industry. And San Diego is a Southern Californian city sitting on the ocean.

(www.koreatimes.co.kr)

입국이 거절된 승객은?

유명 가수 유승준 씨가 우리나라에 입국하지 못하고 다시 로스앤젤레스로 돌아갔던 일이 있다. 국제선 승객은 목적지 국가로 여행하기 위한 적법한 여행 관련 서류를 공항에서 항공사 직원에게 제시하게 되어 있다. 적법한 여행서류는 각 국가 간의 협정 사항으로 보통 여권, 비자 등이 주된 내용이다.

유씨의 경우는 미국 시민권자로 미국 여권을 소지했다. 미국 여권 소지자는 단순 방문의 경우 왕복 항공권이 있다면 비자 없이도 30일간 한국에 머무를 수 있지만 그의 입국이 거부된 것은 특수한 사정에 의해서였다.

즉, 한국에 입국하기 위한 여행 서류가 미비해서가 아니라 당국에서 입국이 '국가 이익에 반하는 것'으로 판명했기 때문이다.

우리나라 출입국관리법 제76조 3항에 의하면 외국에서 입국하는 승객이 한국에서 입국을 거절당할 경우, 그 승객을 모시고 온 항공사가 원래 출발지로 가장 빠른 항공편을 이용하여 그 승객을 수송해야 하는 책임이 있다.

이 경우, 출입국 관리사무소는 입국거절 승객에 대한 송환 지시서를 발급하게 되는데 항공사는 승객 수송 후 이를 이행했다는 증빙 서류를 제출해야 한다. 이런 규정은 모든 나라가 대동소이하게 적용하고 있다.

따라서 입국거절 승객을 탑승시켜야 하는 책임은 해당 항공사에 있다. 그런데 항공 좌석이 만석이거나 당일 돌아가는 항공편이 없을 경우에는 어떻게 될까? 만석인 경우에는 대기자 중 최우선 순위를 부여, 우선적으로 탑승할 수 있도록 조치하며 때로는 예약 승객에게 양해를 구하고 탑승시키기도 한다. 또 항공기 스케줄 등의 문제로 당일 소환이 불가능한 경우에는 공항 내 감호소에 보호하거나 항공사 관리 아래 가입국 조치를 시킨 뒤 다음날 송환하기도 한다.

입국거절 승객의 발생 비용(항공 요금, 일시 보호비 등)은 당연히 승객이 부담해야 한다. 하지만 항공권도 없고 이를 구입할 만한 비용도 없을 경우에는 우선 해당 항공사가 요금을 부담하고 추후 승객으로부터 회수하게 된다.

비엔나국제공항 *Vienna International Airport*

동유럽으로 연결되는 최적의 공항이라는 위치를 강조하는 Vienna International Airport

Unit 06

Please take me to the Monte Hotel

06 Please take me to the Monte Hotel

Before we go

- What do you think of public transportation in Seoul?
- Have you ever taken a taxi in a foreign country?
- How often do you take a taxi?

Words and phrases

- take a bus/taxi/subway
- dollar/cent
- arrive
- change
- tip

Taking a taxi CD TRACK 1

Taxi driver : Where to, ma'am?

Chae-rim : **Please take me to the Monte Hotel.**

Taxi driver : Yes, ma'am.

(They are arriving at the Monte Hotel.)

Chae-rim : **How much do I owe you?**

Taxi driver : That's 13 dollars and 25 cents.

Chae-rim : Here is 15 dollars. Please keep the change.

Taking a bus CD TRACK 2

Chae-rim : Excuse me. Does this bus go to Manhattan?

Bus driver : No, it doesn't. It goes to Brooklyn.

Chae-rim : **Can you tell me which bus goes to Manhattan?**

Bus driver : Take the bus No. 152.

Chae-rim : Thank you.

Asking for directions (1) CD TRACK 3

Chae-rim : **Can you tell me how to get to** Central Park?

Pedestrian : Yes. Go straight and turn left onto Grand Street. Walk two blocks to Central Avenue. **You will see** the park on the left.

Chae-rim : I'm sorry but I didn't get that. Could you say that again, please?

Pedestrian : Okay. First, go straight and turn left onto Grand Street. Are you following me so far?

Chae-rim : Yes.

Pedestrian : Then two blocks to Central Avenue. The park is on the left. **You can't miss it.**

Chae-rim : Now I've got it. Thanks a lot.

Asking direction (2) CD TRACK 4

Chae-rim : Good morning. Can you help me? I'm looking for a travel agent to change my ticket.

Johnson : Certainly, ma'am. Go out of this building, turn right, go along this Olympic Avenue about 100 meters, and there are two travel agents on the left.

Chae-rim : So, go out of this building, turn right and along Olympic Ave for 100 meters.

Johnson : That's right.

Chae-rim : Thank you so much.

Johnson : It's my pleasure.

Asking direction (3) CD TRACK 5

Chae-rim : Can you tell me where the nearest bank is?

Heather : It's not far. It is just a few minutes walk. Go out of the hotel, turn right, go along 3rd street to 5th street, then turn right and go up Fairfax Ave until you get to Alhambra Ave. The bank is at the corner on your right.

Chae-rim : So that's out of the hotel, right and straight up to Alhambra Ave.

Heather : Yes, and the bank's right at the corner.

Chae-rim : Thank you very much.

Grammar point

Take + 사람 + to + 장소 ~를 어디로 데려가다

흔히 일상대화에서 많이 쓰이는 표현이다.

- **Take me to the park.**
  공원으로 데려다 주세요.
- **I will take you to the Disney Land this summer.**
  이번 여름에 디즈니랜드에 데려갈게.

등 여러 표현을 쓸 수 있다. 명심할 것은 take 다음에 나오는 사람은 항상 목적격 인칭대명사를 써야 한다.

주격(~이, ~가)	목적격(~을, ~를)	소유격(~의)	소유대명사(~의 것)
I	me	my	mine
you	you	your	yours
he	him	his	his
she	her	her	hers
it	it	its	its
they	them	their	theirs
we	us	our	ours

Expression

How much do I owe you?

'owe'의 사전적 의미는 '빚지다'라는 뜻이다. 직역을 하면 영어권 사람들은 '얼마예요?'라는 표현으로 "얼마의 빚을 진 거지요?(How much do I owe you?)"라고 물어본다. 간단히 "How much?"라고 표현해도 된다.

Can you tell me how to get to 장소~

길을 물어보는 표현이다.

Do you know how to get to 장소~
Can you show me how to get to 장소~

Language focus

to / from, into / out of, on / off, etc.

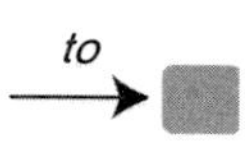

Andy is going **to** New York next week.
We walked **from** the hotel to the restaurant.

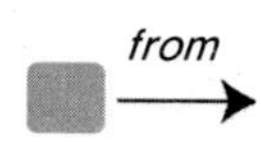

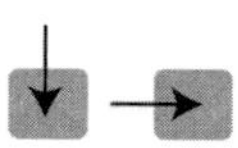

into(in)

David jumped **into** the water.
I came **out of** the house and got **into** a car.

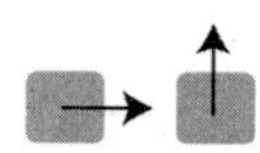

out of

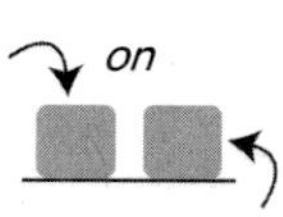

Don't put your feet **on** the table.
Take your feet **off** the table.
She is hanging some pictures **on** the wall

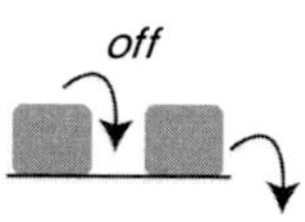

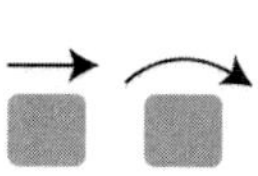

over

The plane flew **over** the mountains.
I climbed **over** the wall into the yard.
Some people say it is unlucky to walk **under** a ladder.

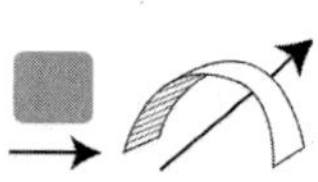

under

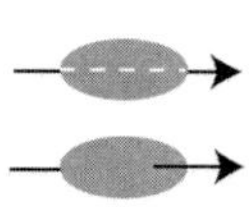

through

A bird flew into the room **through** a window.
This street goes **through** the city.
This street goes **around** the city.
The bus stop is just **around** the corner.

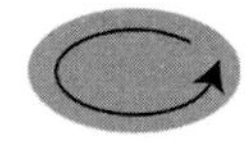

around the town

town around

Practice

Complete the sentences with the words to/over/out of, etc.

1. I looked .... the window and watched the people in the street.
2. My house is very near here. It's just .... the corner.
3. Do you know how to put batteries .... the camera?
4. How far is it .... here .... the airport?
5. She took a key .... her bag and opened the door.

Exercise

1. 어디로 모실까요?

----

2. 롯데백화점에 데려다 주실 수 있으세요?

----

3. 물론이지요.

----

4. 요금은 얼마인가요?

----

5. 죄송합니다. 다시 한번 말씀해 주시겠어요?

----

6. 잔돈은 가지세요.

----

7. 서울역으로 가려면 어떻게 가야 합니까?

----

8. 사당역에서 4호선으로 갈아타세요.

Discussion

Should we spend more money on improving roads and highways or on improving public transportation such as buses and subways?

A : I think we should spend more money on public transportation.

B : Why do you think so?

A : Because public transportation is of great benefit to all of us.

B : What you're saying is a little bit vague to me.

A : What I meant is everyone can take advantage of an improved public transportation system whereas only the driver benefits from better roads.

B : That makes sense.

A : In addition, if more and more people use public transport because it is easy and pleasant to use, traffic problems will be reduced.

B : Let's see this issue in terms of the protection of the environment, then. Do you think public transportation is more environmentally friendly than cars?

A : Well... I haven't thought about it. **I think I would have to think about it more.**

도로나 고속도로를 개발하는 데 재정을 써야 할까, 버스나 지하철 같은 대중교통 수단을 위해 재정을 써야 할까?

A : 저는 대중교통에 좀 더 많은 돈을 써야 한다고 생각해요.

B : 왜 그렇게 생각하세요?

A : 왜냐면 대중교통은 우리 모두에게 이익을 줄 수 있기 때문이죠.

B : 말씀하시는 게 약간 불분명하네요.

A : 제 말은, 도로를 개발하면 운전자에게만 좋겠지만 대중교통을 개발하면 모든 사람에게 유용하다는 말이예요.

B : 맞는 말이네요.

A : 게다가 대중교통이 편리하고 깨끗하다면 더 많은 사람들이 대중교통을 이용할 테고 그러면 교통문제도 줄일 수 있죠.

B : 그러면, 환경보호의 측면에서 이 문제를 다뤄보도록 합시다. 대중교통이 자동차보다 좀 더 환경친화적이라고 생각하세요?

A : 글쎄요... 이 문제에 대해서는 한 번도 생각해 본 적이 없어요. **이것에 대해 좀 더 생각해 봐야 할 것 같아요.**

Tip

I think I would have to think about it more.
이 문제에 대해 좀 더 생각해 봐야 할 것 같아요.

어떤 주제에 대해 좀 더 시간을 갖고 생각해 봐야 할 때 쓰는 표현이다.

- I think I need more time to think about it.
- I think I have to sleep on it.
- Would you give me more time to think about it?
- I have to study about it.

Topics for further discussion

❶ On what occasion do you usually take a taxi?

❷ Among automobiles, bicycles, and airplanes, which do you think changed people's lives most?

❸ Do you feel safe when you take a bus or taxi? Why or why not?

차이나월드호텔*China World Hotel*

호텔 광고에서 고려하여야 하는 주요 요인(종사원, 시설, 약속이행 등)을 훌륭하게 전달하고 있는 차이나월드호텔

Unit 07

I have a reservation here.

07 *I have a reservation here.*

Before we go

- What type of hotel do you want to stay in during your honeymoon?
- Which do you prefer to stay, in a hotel or a resort?

Words and phrases

- I have a reservation here
- smoking or non-smoking floor
- exchange
- currency
- registration form
- wake-up call
- extra charge
- cash or charge

Check in (1) CD TRACK 1

Clerk : Welcome to the Hilton. May I help you, ma'am?

Chae-rim : I'd like to check in. **I have a reservation here.**

Clerk : May I have your name, please?

Chae-rim : Chae-rim Lee.

Clerk : Yes, Ms. Lee. I see your name on the reservation list. You requested a single room for three nights, is that correct?

Chae-rim : Yes, could I have a room on the upper floors away from the ice machine, please?

Clerk : No problem, ma'am. Do you prefer a smoking or non-smoking floor?

Chae-rim : Non-smoking please.

Clerk : **Could you fill out the registration form,** please... Thank you. **And how would you like to pay, cash or charge?**

Chae-rim : I'm going to pay cash when I check-out.

Clerk : Yes, ma'am. Your room number is 1001

	and here's your key. If you require anything further, feel free to call the front desk. Would you like assistance with your bags?
Chae-rim :	No thanks, I only have one. I can manage it. And I'd like to leave wake up call for 7:00 am.
Clerk :	Certainly, Ms. Lee. Enjoy your stay!

Check in (2) CD TRACK 2

Receptionist :	Good afternoon, sir. May I help you?
Guest :	Yes. I want to check in, please.
Receptionist :	Do you have a reservation, sir?
Guest :	I have a reservation for two nights.
Receptionist :	May I have your name or confirmation number please?
Guest :	My name is Min-Ho Kim.
Receptionist :	Just a moment, Mr. Kim. I'll check the list. Thank you for waiting. We have your reservation. You'll stay here for 2 nights from July 20th, won't you?

Guest: Right.

Receptionist: May I see your picture ID and credit card, please?

Guest: All right. Here you go.

Receptionist: By the way, did you request an extra bed?

Guest: Yes, I did.

Receptionist: We'll arrange an extra bed in your room. And there will be an extra charge of $15 for it.

Guest: Yes, I heard that when I booked. That's fine with me.

Receptionist: Mr. Kim. Here is your key. Your room number is 1201. Our bell staff will help you with your luggage in your room. If you have any questions about our facilities, please call the front desk anytime.

Guest: Thank you! Have a nice day!

Receptionist: Thank you. Have a pleasant stay, Mr. Kim.

Check in (3) CD TRACK 3

Hotel clerk : Good afternoon, ma'am. May I help you?

Chae-rim : I have a reservation here for two nights. I called on June 20th from Korea.

Hotel clerk : May I have your name?

Chae-rim : My name is Chae-rim Lee. Lee is my family name.

Hotel clerk : Just a moment, please. Oh, yes. We have your reservation. You will stay here from July 20th to the 22nd, won't you?

Chae-rim : Yes. That's right.

Hotel clerk : Here's your key. Your room number is 1145. Our bellboy will carry your baggage.

Chae-rim : Thank you.

Grammar point

부가의문문

You will stay here, won't you? 여기 머무실 거예요, 그렇죠?

앞에서 말한 것을 확인하거나 상대방의 동의를 구하고자 할 때 평서문 뒤에 덧붙여서 쓰는 것을 부가의문문이라고 한다.

부가의문문 만드는 법

형 태	• 긍정문 뒤에는 부정형(항상 단축형) • 부정문 뒤에는 긍정형
주 어	• 대명사
동 사	• be 동사/조동사 → 그대로 • 일반동사 → do, does, did 중 하나

- You like pizza, don't you?
- He is not a student, is he?
- They can play the piano, can't they?

Expression

How would you like to pay?

상점에서 물건 값을 지불하거나 서비스 이용 요금을 지불할 때 “어떻게(무엇으로) 계산하시겠습니까?”라고 묻는 표현으로 “How would you like to pay?”가 가장 대표적이다. 그 외에도 간단히 “Cash or charge?”라고도 많이 사용한다.
‘charge’는 동사로 ‘담다, 채우다, 지우다’의 의미로 쓰이는 경우가 대부분인데, 여기서는 명사로 credit card(신용카드)를 의미한다. 미국인들은 이 말을 빠르게 발음하므로 charge라는 단어를 사전에 알아두지 않으면 이해하기 어렵다.
요즘은 신용카드 사용 시 할부로 많이 사용한다. 영어 표현에서 할부 계산은 “buy ~ on a three-month installment plan”에서 기간만 바꾸어 쓰면 된다.

Can I pay in installments?
할부로 되나요?
On a six-month installment plan, is it okay?
6개월 할부가 가능합니다. 괜찮으시겠어요?

Exercise

1. 안녕하세요. 제 이름은 박민철이고요. 5일 동안 머물 방을 예약했습니다.

2. 잠시만 기다려 주세요. 네, 예약하신 방이 있네요. 11월 12일에서 16일까지 머무실 거네요. 그렇지요?

3. 네 맞아요.

4. 1324호입니다. 키는 여기 있어요.

5. 벨보이가 당신의 짐을 운반해줄 것입니다.

6. 궁금하신 점이 있으시면, 언제든지 객실부로 연락주세요.

7. 내일 오전 7시에 기상전화를 받고 싶습니다.

Discussion

Do you think visiting a country is always the best way to learn about that country?

A: I believe we have to visit a country if we want to know that country.

B: I **am not sure but** reading books about a country can be another way.

A: You're right, but visiting and experiencing the country make you understand the foreign country more clearly and thoroughly. So, people say experience is the best teacher. My dream is to be a good teacher with experience. What is yours?

B: What are you talking about? **That's beside the point.**

어느 나라를 배우는 최고의 방법은 그 나라를 방문하는 것이라고 생각하는가?

A: 저는 한 나라를 알고자 한다면, 그 나라를 방문해야 한다고 생각합니다.

B: **확실히 모르겠지만,** 그 나라에 대해 책을 읽는 것도 다른 방법이 될 수 있을 것 같은데요.

A: 맞아요. 하지만 그 나라를 직접 가보고 경험해 봐야 다른 나라를 좀 더 명확하고 완전히 이해할 수 있어요. 그래서 경험이 최고의 교사라는 말도 있잖아요. 경험이 풍부한 교사가 되는 게 제 꿈이에요. 당신 꿈은 무엇인가요?

B: 도대체 무슨 말씀이세요? **논지에서 벗어나는 얘기네요.**

Tip

I am not sure but 확실하지는 않지만

자신의 의견에 확신이 서지 않을 때 쓸 수 있는 표현이다.

- I am not confident but...
- I don't know much about this, but...

That's beside the point. 요점에서 벗어나는 얘기네요.

토론을 하다 보면 처음에는 하나의 토론 주제에서 시작했으나 다른 이야기로 주제가 흘러가거나 토론자가 토론 주제와는 상관없는 논리를 펼 때가 있다. 그 때 주의를 줄 수 있는 표현이 "That's the beside the point."이다.

- You're missing the point.
- I think what you are saying is out of the point.

Topics for further discussion

❶ How much would you be willing to pay to stay at a five-star hotel?

❷ Would you call the police if a stranger entered your room without your permission?

❸ What would you do if you had to share a room with a heavy snorer?

포 시즌스*Four Seasons Hotels and Resorts*

트레블러(Traveler), 에어라인 비즈니스(Airline Business) 등의 세계적 여행 잡지가 선정하는 세계 최고의 리조트호텔로 매년 선정되고 있는 포 시즌스 호텔은 고객의 욕구를 만족시키는 세심한 서비스로 좋은 평가를 받고 있다.

Unit 08

Is there any place where I can use the Internet?

08 Is there any place where I can use the Internet?

Before we go

- What types of amenities do you use in hotels?
- If you have some free time in a hotel, what are you going to do first?

Words and phrases

- business center
- in-room facility
- Internet access
- concierge
- extra charge
- indoor/outdoor
- gym

Business center (1)

CD TRACK 1

Chae-rim : Can you tell me about your in-room facilities?

Receptionist : Of course. All rooms have satellite TV with pay-per-view so that you can watch films, play games, and listen to music. There's Internet access for sending emails, accessing websites, and for finding out information about the hotel, for example, services, facilities, and car hire. Both the minibar and the electronic safe are standard in all rooms. We have 24-hour room service and a babysitting service...

Chae-rim : What about facilities for business travellers?

Receptionist : All the rooms have multi-line phones. But the printer, photocopier, and fax facilities are in the business center just opposite the reception. The center's fully equipped and offers broadband Internet access.

08

Business center (2) CD TRACK 2

Guest: I need to check my emails but I forgot to bring my laptop. **Is there any place where I can use the Internet around here?**

Staff: Certainly, sir. The Business Center at the hotel has Internet access.

Guest: **That sounds good.** I can check some information for a meeting.

Staff: Absolutely, sir. The Business Center opens at 10 in the morning and closes at 11:30 in the evening.

Guest: Do you know how much it costs?

Staff: It will be 10 dollars an hour to use the Internet.

Guest: WOW, it's not cheap. By the way, can I send and receive a fax in the Business Center, too?

Staff: Unfortunately, you can use fax services at the front desk or concierge, only.

Guest: Alright, thanks for your help.

Staff: My pleasure, sir.

Asking the concierge for restaurant advice

CD TRACK 3

Chae-rim' friend : I need a suggestion for a restaurant here in Manhattan.

Concierge : Certainly! How much do you plan to spend on dinner, sir?

Chae-rim' friend : My date is very sophisticated, so I'm sure she would expect nothing but the best.

Concierge : May I suggest our own hotel restaurant? It's got five stars in the latest restaurant review.

Chae-rim' friend : No, thank you, I was there last night and I want to go out on the town this time. What other ideas do you have?

Concierge : There's always Gramercy Tavern. They have live jazz and delicious food, but very expensive.

Chae-rim' friend : That sounds like a good place to take a date. Can you make a reservation for us?

Concierge : As you wish, sir. You'll have a wonderful time there.

Laundry service

CD TRACK 4

Staff: Good afternoon! This is Room Service. Can I help you?

Chae-rim: Yes, please. Could you send someone up to my room, please. I have some laundry to be washed. My room number is 1001.

Staff: Sure, I will send a maid to your room shortly, anything else?

Chae-rim: I want to know how long it will take to get the laundry done.

Staff: It takes at least a day, so your item will be delivered in the morning the day after tomorrow. Is that okay with you, ma'am?

Chae-rim: That will be fine. Thanks.

Staff: Have a nice day, ma'am.

Grammar point

미국식 영어 vs 영국식 영어

미국 영어와 영국 영어는 발음이 많이 다르며 뜻은 같아도 철자는 다른 단어를 많이 사용한다.

미국식	영국식	단어의 뜻
color	colour	색 깔
center	centre	중 심
exit	way out	출 구
subway	underground	지하철
French fries	chips	감자튀김
cab	taxi	택 시
fall	autumn	가 을
parking lot	car park	주차장
drugstore	chemist	약 국
gas/gasoline	petrol	휘발유
movie	cinema	영 화
vacation	holiday	휴 일

Expression

감탄사(Interjection)

Oops! 어이쿠
Well/Gee... 글쎄
Oh, my gosh 맙소사(당황/놀람)
Yahoo 야호
Bless you 행운이 있길
Wow 와우

Language focus

adverbs of frequency always / usually / often etc.

We often use these adverbs with the verb in the middle of a sentence.

always	*often*	*ever*	*rarely*
usually	*sometimes*	*never*	*seldom*

- Always/never etc., usually go <u>before</u> the verb.
  I *always go* to work by subway.
  She *often plays* tennis.
  They *usually have* dinner at 7 o'clock.

- Always/never, etc., go <u>after</u> am/is/are/was/were.
  I *am usually* at home in the evening.
  It *is often* very cold here in the winter.

- Always/never, etc., go <u>between</u> two verbs(have... been/can... find, etc.)
  I *will always remember* you.
  Have you *ever been* to Greece?

Practice

Write the sentences with the words in parentheses( ).

1. Ashley is polite. (always) Ashley *is always polite* ....
2. I go to bed before midnight. (rarely) I ....
3. I will forget what you said. (never) I ....
4. Heather doesn't work on Saturdays. (usually) She ....
5. Have you been to Hawaii. (ever) ....
6. What do you have for breakfast? (usually) ....

Exercise

1. 방안의 시설들에 대해 설명해 주시겠어요?

----

2. 비즈니스센터에서 인터넷을 이용하실 수 있습니다.

----

3. 반가운 말씀이네요.

----

4. 가격이 얼마인지 아십니까?

----

5. 저녁으로 어느 정도 돈을 지불하실 생각이신지요?

----

6. 당신의 물건은 내일 오전까지 배달될 것입니다.

----

7. 제 방으로 직원 한 분을 올려 보내주시겠습니까?

Discussion

If you are to go on a trip for a year, what would you take with you?

A : If you are to go on a trip for a year, what would you take?

B : It's a tough question. Well... I would take my laptop computer with me.

A : **Do you have any reason** to take a laptop computer?

B : **First of all,** I can keep in touch with my family and friends by sending emails. Secondly, I can see what is going on in Korea by surfing Korean news websites. Finally, I can also play computer games.

A : You'd better think again. What if you travel to a country where the Internet is not available?

B : You're right. I didn't consider that. Then what will you take if you go on a long trip?

A : I will take my diary. I will write every interesting thing that I see and all the feelings that I experience during the trip.

B : That's a good idea.

A : When I came back to Korea, I can publish my trip diary. Who knows? It could be a best seller and I could be a millionaire!!

1년 정도 여행을 떠난다면 무엇을 가져가겠는가?

A : 1년 정도 여행을 떠난다면 무엇을 가져가겠어요?

B : 어려운 질문이네요. 음 저는 노트북을 가져가겠어요.

A : 노트북을 가져가는 **이유라도 있나요?**

B : **우선,** 이메일을 주고받으면 가족들과 계속해서 연락할 수 있습니다. 두 번째로는 한국 뉴스 사이트를 서핑하면 한국에서 무슨 일이 일어나고 있는지 여행 중에도 알 수 있지요. 마지막으로, 컴퓨터 게임도 할 수 있고요.

A : 다시 생각해 보셔야 할 것 같네요. 만약 인터넷 연결이 안 되는 곳으로 여행을 가신다면요?

B : 그러네요. 그건 생각해 보지 않았네요. 그렇다면 당신은 무엇을 가져가시겠어요?

A : 저는 일기장을 가져가겠어요. 여행 동안 제가 보고 느꼈던 모든 흥미로운 것을 다 적으려고요.

B : 좋은 생각이예요.

A : 한국에 돌아온 후 여행 일기를 출판할 수도 있겠지요. 누가 알아요? 책이 베스트셀러가 되서 제가 백만장자가 될지.

Tip

Do you have any reason to~ ~하는 이유가 있나요?

앞에서 토론자가 얘기한 것에 대해 구체적인 이유를 물어볼 때 쓰는 표현이다. 토론할 때는 자신의 의견과 그 의견을 뒷받침하는 구체적인 이유를 밝혀야 하므로 토론자의 주장에 충분한 이유나 근거가 없다고 생각할 때는 언제든지 구체적인 이유를 물어볼 수 있다.

- Is there any particular reason to~ ~하는 특별한 이유라도 있나요?
- Why do you~ 왜 ~하시나요?

First of all

자신의 의견을 논리적 이유로 설명할 때, 그 이유가 여러 가지라면 first of all(우선은), secondly(두 번째로는), finally(마지막으로는)는 사용하여 주장의 논리적 근거를 댈 수 있다.

You'd better think again, I think. 좀 더 생각해 보셔야 할 것 같은데요.

상대방에게 제시한 의견을 다시 한번 고려해 줄 것을 요구할 때 쓰는 표현이다.

- I think you have to think about it a bit more.
- I am sure you have to think it over.
- Please reconsider it.
- Why don't you think it over?

Topics for further discussion

❶ Why are business travelers so important to travel agents, airlines and hotels?

❷ What kind of hotel is a business traveler likely to stay in?

❸ What facilities are important to you when choosing a hotel?

Reading

Hawaii hotels post weakest summer ever

Hotels in Hawaii had their weakest summer on record－an average of 68.1 percent occupancy－according to a report released today. Revenue per room has also plummeted as hotels lower rates to lure guests, said Joseph Toy, Hospitality Advisors LLC president and chief executive officer. Occupancy for June, July and August was the lowest since Hospitality Advisors began conducting its survey in 1987, and compares with rates in the mid-80 percent range in the summer just three years ago.

The statewide average daily room rate fell by 15.9 percent to $177.79 for August－the latest available statistics－resulting in a 19.9 percent decline in revenue per available room to $126.05. The hotel industry lost an estimated $238 million in total revenue－including revenue from rooms, food and beverage and retail sales－this summer compared with 2008, Toy said. And the drop is even more dramatic－$374 million when compared with the boom tourism summer of 2006.

"Summer is obviously one of the most important times of the year," Towill said. "So being down over $230 million is a big hit." Towill said some companies have been able to schedule renovations while others don't have the resources amid the recession. For Aqua Hotels & Resorts, the challenging year has been an opportunity to expand from a Waikiki-based management business with about a dozen hotels on O'ahu to 16 hotels on four islands.

"The one good thing about a down market is the chance to expand," said Ben Rafter, president and chief executive officer of Aqua Hotels & Resorts.

"It's a great time to be a consumer with a little bit of spending money." Rafter predicts that occupancy will level off and stabilize but rates may drop more.

"We just have to figure out how to grow the market again," Rafter said. He predicted a rebound by late 2010 and 2011.

O'ahu posted the highest August 2009 occupancy of all the Islands at 78.3 percent, with Waikiki achieving hotel occupancies above 80 percent. O'ahu luxury hotels also posted the highest occupancy by price class at 83.3 percent.

However, the overall average daily rate for O'ahu fell 15.7 percent to $177.36 for the month. Maui continued to lead the market for the average daily rate at $231.67, but suffered the largest rate loss of 19.6 percent.

Occupancy for Maui also fell by 2.9 percentage points to 66.2 percent. The island of Hawaii recorded an average daily rate of $193.68, or 8.6 percent lower than a year ago. The Big Island also recorded the lowest island hotel occupancy at 57.2 percent. Kaua'i averaged 65.8 percent occupancy with an average daily rate of $190.78, or 8.4 percentage points and 12.1 percent behind the prior year, respectively. Luxury hotels led all segments in both occupancy and average daily rate at 77.7 percent and $252.35, but were down 3.0 percentage points and 18.1 percent, respectively, from last year. Midprice and economy hotels tied for the lowest occupancy among statewide price classes at 61.3 percent. For August 2009, the survey included 159 properties representing 47,083 rooms, or 83.2 percent of all lodging properties with 20 rooms or more.

(based on Oct. 9, honoluluadvertiser.com)

08

Is there any place where I can use the Internet?

호텔팩, 에어텔, 패키지?

호텔팩과 패키지 상품의 다른 점은 개인 여행자에게 적당한 프로그램이냐 아니면 단체 여행객에게 적당한 상품이냐다. 즉, 호텔팩은 호텔에서의 숙박과 식사(보통 조식만 포함)를 기본으로 하고 여기에 호텔 내의 일정한 부대시설을 무료로 이용할 수 있도록 프로그램이 구성되어 있는 것이 보통이다. 호텔에서 판매하는 상품이기 때문에 정규 요금으로 투숙할 때보다 다소 저렴하게 구성되는데, 특히 아이가 동반된 가족인 경우, 아이에 해당하는 요금을 저렴하게 책정하는 경우도 있다. 호텔팩은 한마디로 가족끼리, 혹은 부부끼리, 친구끼리 편안하게 지내기 위해 상품을 선택하는 경우에 유효하다. 다른 사람들로부터 방해받지 않고 여행할 수 있다는 장점이 있긴 하지만 개인 여행자를 위한 프로그램이기 때문에 패키지 상품의 가격보다 다소 비싼 것은 감수해야 한다. 비싼 만큼의 반대급부를 얻기 때문이다.

반면, 여행사의 패키지 상품을 구매하여 여행하는 사람들에게도 장·단점은 있다. 호텔팩을 구입하는 사람들의 경우, 호텔 투숙 이외에 주변을 둘러보고 싶다면 스스로 렌터카를 하거나 현지 여행사의 상품을 구매해서 여행해야 하는 불편함이 있지만 패키지 상품을 구입하면 매일 매일의 모든 일정이 정해져 있기 때문에 가이드가 안내하는 곳으로만 따라다니면 된다. 하지만 패키지 상품의 단점은 현지에서 행사를 진행하는 여행사들이 그들의 이윤을 높여야 하기 때문에 여행객들을 쇼핑센터로 안내하는 비율이 높거나 시간 배정을 길게 잡는 등 옵션 상품을 강매 또는 강요하는 경우가 있어 여행객들이 피해를 보는 사례도 있다.

최근엔 에어텔을 선호하는 사람들이 늘고 있다. 호텔이나 여행사에서 호텔팩을 판매하는 것과 마찬가지로 항공사나 그 항공사를 이용하는 여행사에서 에어텔 상품을 구매할 수 있다. 에어텔은 보통 항공사에서 항공편과 현지의 호텔(보통 조식 포함), 때에 따라서는 렌터카 할인 혜택까지 부여하는 상품으로 구성하여 선보이는 경우가 보통이다.

하얏트 리조트*Hyatt Resorts*

최근에는 휴양과 피서 그리고 스포츠 등이 결합된 리조트의 인기가 높아지고 있다.

Unit 09

I'd like to make a collect call to Seoul.

09 *I'd like to make a collect call to Seoul.*

Before we go

- To whom do you give a call most frequently? For what?
- Do you like sending text messages with your cellular phone?
- What do you do when you call a wrong number?

Words and phrases

- operator
- collect call
- party
- go ahead
- leave a message
- take a message
- appreciate

Making a collect call CD TRACK 1

Operator : Operator. Can I help you?

Chae-rim : Yes, please. **I'd like to make a collect call to Seoul, Korea.**

Operator : What's the name of the party and the number, please?

Chae-rim : I want to call Jun-hee Lee, and his number is 82-2-277-6993.

Operator : Just a second, please

(After a while)

Operator : Hello, this is the operator. Your party is on the line. Go ahead.

Chae-rim : Thanks.

Jun-hee : Hi, Chae-rim, How are you?

Chae-rim : I am fine, thanks.

Jun-hee : Chae-rim, listen. I can't talk right now. I am taking a shower. **Can you give me a call later?**

Chae-rim : Oh, sure. I will call you later.

Leaving a message

CD TRACK 2

Chae-rim : May I speak to Mr. Park, please?

Joshua : **Who is calling, please?**

Chae-rim : This is Chae-rim speaking.

Joshua : Hold on, please. I'm afraid he is out. **Would you like to leave a message?**

Chae-rim : Yes. Please tell him that Chae-rim called from New York.

Joshua : All right. I'll give him your message.

Chae-rim : Thank you. I appreciate it.

Grammar point

To 부정사

I want to call Jun-hee Lee.

"나는 새 자동차를 원해"와 같은 문장은 영어로 "I want a new car."가 될 것이다. 그러나 "새 자동차를 갖고 싶다"고 표현하고 싶다면 "I want to get a new car."로 표현할 수 있다. 즉, want라는 동사는 to 부정사를 목적어로 갖는다.

to 부정사 란 'to+동사원형'의 형태를 말한다.
다음 동사들도 want 동사와 동일하게 to 부정사를 목적어로 취한다.

- I decided to sell his old car.
- I hope to see you again.
- She plans to go to LA.
- They wish to be alone.

반면, 목적어로 to 부정사가 아닌 **동명사** (동사+~ing)를 취하는 동사도 있다.

- I enjoy reading a book.
- James finished studying.
- I don't mind eating out.
- My father couldn't give up smoking in a day.

Expression

Give me a call later.

'전화를 걸다'라는 표현은 'call'이라는 동사로 간단히 표현할 수 있다. "전화를 해 달라"고 말할 때 다음처럼 표현할 수 있다.

Ring me up.	Give me a call.
Give me a ring.	Phone me.

May I speak to Ms. Park, please?

'~를 바꿔 달라'를 평범하게 쓸 수 있는 표현이 'May I speak to+사람'이다. 이 외에도 "Is there Ms. Park?" 혹은 "Can I talk to Ms. Park?"처럼 쓸 수 있으며, 간단히 "Ms. Park, please."라고 말할 수도 있다.

Would you like to leave a message?

'leave a message'는 '메시지를 남기다'라는 뜻이고 'take a message'는 '메시지를 받다'라는 뜻이다. 따라서 "메시지를 남기시겠어요?"라고 물어볼 때, 'leave' 동사를 쓰면 말하는 상대방에게 물어보는 것이므로, "Will you leave a message?"라고 표현하고, 'take' 동사를 쓰면 화자가 주어가 되어 "Can I take your message?"라고 표현한다.

Exercise

1. Smith씨 좀 바꿔주세요.

---

2. 지금 잠시 외출 중이신데요.

---

3. 뉴욕에서 채림이 전화했었다고 메모 남겨주세요.

---

4. 메시지를 받아드릴까요? 아니면 전화번호를 남기시겠어요?

---

5. 아니오, 괜찮아요. 제가 다시 전화드릴게요.

Discussion

What is your favorite method of communication among letters, emails, telephone, and face-to-face communication?

A : What is your favorite method of communication, letters, emails, telephone, or face-to-face?

B : Speaking of the communication method, I think face to face communication is the best of all.

A : That's interesting. Why do you think so?

B : Communication is not merely words and letters. Intonation, tone of the voice, and body language are also significant.

A : **Go on.**

B : When someone misunderstands something, I can know it immediately and remove the misunderstanding.

A : You're right. I thought that the email is best because it is convenient and cheap. Though, **I can see your point of view is reasonable.**

선호 의사소통 수단

A : 편지, 이메일, 전화나 직접 만나서 얘기하는 것 중 선호하는 의사소통 방법은 무엇인가요?

B : 의사소통 방법에 대해 얘기하자면, 저는 직접 만나서 얘기하는 것이 최고라고 생각해요.

A : 흥미롭군요. 왜 그렇게 생각하세요?

B : 의사소통은 단순히 말이나 단어의 단순한 나열은 아니지요. 억양이나, 목소리 톤, 바디 랭귀지도 어떤 의미를 전달하지요.

A : **계속해 보세요.**

B : 누군가가 제 말을 오해했을 때, 오해를 바로 풀 수도 있고요.

A : 맞아요. 저는 이메일이 간편함과 저렴함을 이유로 최고의 의사소통 수단이라고 생각했는데, **당신 관점도 타당하네요.**

Tip

Go on. 계속 하세요.

자신이 상대방의 말을 잘 듣고 있음을 상대에게 확인시켜 주는 표현이다.

- I am listening.
- I am all ears.
- I am with you.
- I am following you.
- I understand so far.

I can see your point of view is reasonable. 말씀하시는 것이 타당하네요.

토론자는 상대방의 의견이 나와 다르더라도 상대의 의견이 타당할 때는 그 타당성을 인정하는 것이 중요하다. 상대 의견의 타당성을 인정할 때 쓰는 표현이다.

- What you are saying makes sense. 타당한 말씀이시네요.
- Your saying can be right. 말씀하시는 게 맞는 것 같아요.

Topics for further discussion

❶ Do you think that university students need cellular phones? Can you give me reasons that support your idea?

❷ How much do you spend on your phone bill? Do you think you are spending a moderate amount of money on phone service?

Reading

Jeju as a global tourist haven

Korean nationals will be able to buy up to $1,200 worth of goods a year at duty-free shops on the southern island of Jeju, under an ambitious plan to turn the island into an international free city.

These are among the highlights of the finalized and long-disputed plan to make the southernmost scenic island of Jeju an international free city

The basis of the envisioned bill is the designation of Jeju International Airport and its vicinity as a tourist and free trade zone, where customs duties will not be imposed and various taxes, like income and corporate taxes, will be reduced or exempted.

Under instructions from President Kim Dae-jung in 1998, the government started working on the Jeju development project, aiming to turn the island into an eco-friendly, visa-free international city like Hong Kong and Singapore.

The government plan will allow visitors from 17 countries, including Vietnam, Mongolia, Cambodia and Pakistan, to enter the island without visas and travel on the mainland to a limited extent.

It also calls for the extension of no-visa tours from the current 15 days to 30, while allowing experts in foreign language education, information and telecommunications, biotechnology and tourism to stay up to five years, up from the present three.

(source from travelinfo.co.kr)

항공기 내 위성전화

통신전자기술의 발달로 고도 30,000피트에서도 일상적인 대화를 할 수 있게 되었다.

Unit 10

Are you ready to order?

10 Are you ready to order?

Before we go

- What kind of food do you like or dislike?
- What do you expect to find on menus in general?
- Do you prefer to pay by credit card or in cash?

Words and phrases

- starters/appetizers/dessert
- main courses
- menu/wine list/dessert menu
- May I take your order/Are you ready to order
- soup of the day/chef's special
- How would you like your steak done
- side dishes
- overcharged/undercharged
- receipt

Greeting customers

CD TRACK 1

Host : Good evening, ma'am. Do you have a reservation?

Chae-rim : No.. but, **do you have a table for two?**

Host : Certainly, ma'am. Would you like smoking or non-smoking?

Chae-rim : Non-smoking, please.

Host : Yes, ma'am. Would you like to follow me, please. There's a table free by the window.

Chae-rim : I'd like that.

Host : If you would like to sit down. Shall I take your coat, ma'am?

Chae-rim : Oh, thank you. Please.

Host : Your waiter Scott will be with you in a minute. If there is anything else I can help you with, please let me know.

Chae-rim : Alright, thank you.

Host : You're welcome and I hope you enjoy your dinner.

10

Taking orders

CD TRACK 2

Waiter : Good evening. I'm Scott, and pleased to be your waiter. **Would you like something to drink** before we start.

Chae-rim : Just some water would be fine.

Waiter : Yes, ma'am. And, here are the menu and wine list. If you would like to have a moment to look at those, I'll be back when you're ready.

Chae-rim : Yes, I guess we'll need some time.

Waiter : Certainly, ma'am. Please let me know whenever you're ready.

Chae-rim : Thank you.

(Chae-rim calls Scott after a few minutes later.)

Waiter : Yes, ma'am. **Are you ready to order?**

Chae-rim : Yes, I think so. But could you tell me what the Soup of the Day is?

Waiter : Certainly. Today we're serving clam chowder soup.

Chae-rim : Sounds good to me, I'll have that. And.., I'll

	have the 16oz Charbroiled Steak. Is it good here?
Waiter :	Oh, yes ma'am, it's the chef's special and I'm sure you would like it.
Chae-rim :	Ok, then I'll have that.
Waiter :	**How would you like your steak done?**
Chae-rim :	Medium will be good for me.
Waiter :	Yes, ma'am. And it comes with a selection of side dishes. We have fries and baked potato.
Chae-rim :	Baked potato with butter and cream, please.
Waiter :	Yes, ma'am. How about you, sir? **May I take your order now?**
Chae-rim's friend :	Yes, let me just have Chicken in White Wine Sauce, please.
Waiter :	Yes, sir.
Waiter :	And what would you like to drink?
Chae-rim's friend :	What would you recommend?
Waiter :	I'd recommend Cabernet Sauvignon.
Chae-rim's friend :	So, we'll have a bottle of that, please.
Waiter :	Thank you. So, that's one Soup of the Day and one plate of the 16oz Charbroiled Steak with baked potato with butter and cream,

	one Chicken in White Wine Sauce, and a bottle of Cabernet Sauvignon.
Chae-rim's friend :	That's right.
Waiter :	Thank you, and I'll be back with your wine.

Payments CD TRACK 3

Waiter :	**Is everything all right?**
Chae-rim's friend :	Yes, everything is good and I really enjoyed the meal.
Waiter :	I'm pleased to hear that. **Would you care for some dessert?**
Chae-rim's friend :	No, we've had enough. Could you just take these dishes away and bring us our check, now?
Waiter :	Certainly, sir. Your check will be ready in just a minute.
Chae-rim's friend :	Thank you.
Waiter :	Excuse me. Here is the check and let me know when you are ready.
Chae-rim's friend :	Well, wait a minute, Scott. I guess you

	overcharged us for the Soup of the Day.
Waiter :	Let me see, please. It says two Soup of the Day...
Chae-rim's friend :	But we had only one of it.
Waiter :	I'm very sorry. I'm afraid there's been a mistake. I'll ask the cashier to deduct one of them.
Chae-rim's friend :	Please.

(Waiter comes back with the new bill)

Waiter :	Thank you for waiting and here is the new bill. I apologize again for the inconvenience.
Chae-rim's friend :	It's OK. Do you accept Visa?
Waiter :	Of course, sir.
Chae-rim's friend :	Good, here is the card.
Waiter :	Thank you, sir. I'll be right back with your receipt.

(Waiter comes back with the receipt a few minutes later.)

Waiter :	Sir. **Can I have your signature** here at the bottom?
Chae-rim's friend :	Sure, here you go.
Waiter :	Thank you very much.

Grammar point

Fraction(분수) / decimal(소수) / Ordinal number(서수) 읽는 법

분수

분모를 서수로, 분자를 기수로 읽는다.

- 1/3 one third
- 2/3 two third
- 3/5 three fifth

소수

소수점 아래는 한 자리씩 읽으며, 소수점은 'point'라고 읽는다.

- 0.008 (zero) point zero zero eight
- 29.76 twenty nine point seven six
- $45.03 forty five dollars and three cents

서수

- 5번가 Fifth Avenue
- 오른쪽에서 3번째 (the) third from the right
- 7층 the seventh floor
- 11월 16일 November sixteenth/(the) sixteenth of November

Expression

Are you ready to order? 주문하시겠습니까?

'order'는 동사로 '명령하다, 지시하다' 또는 명사로 '명령', '지시'의 의미 외에도 동사로 '(상품을) 주문하다, (서비스를) 부탁하다' 또는 '(식당·바 등에서 음식·음료를) 주문하다', 명사로 '주문'이라는 의미를 갖는다. 음식을 주문할 경우에는 'place an order(주문하다)' 또는 'be ready to order(주문할 준비가 되다)'라고 표현한다.

Are you ready to order? May I take your order?
Would you like to place an order?

Would you care for 명사 ~좀 하시겠어요? ~원하세요?

'care for'는 다양한 뜻이 있지만 여기서는 '좋아하다' 또는 '원하다'라는 의미로 쓰인다. "would you care for a drink?"라고 하면 "마실 것을 원하십니까?", "마실 것을 드릴까요?"라는 의미로 "would you like something to drink?"와 같은 의미로 이해하면 된다. 그에 대한 대답으로는 간단히 "Yes, please." 또는 "No, thank you."라고 답하면 된다.

Would you like some candies?	Yes, I'd like peppermint candies.
What would you like to have?	I'd like to have candies.
Would you care for coffee?	Yes, I'd love it.

Language focus

Complaining about food

The following phrases are useful when complaining about food.

- too + adjective(*hot, cold, spicy, salty, slow, expensive etc.*)
  It's *too hot*

- not + adjective enough
  This water *isn't cold enough.*

- There + be not + enough + noun
  There *isn't enough ice.*

- over/under + past participle(*cooked, done, charged etc.*)
  This steak is *undercooked.*

Practice

Complete the sentences with the proper expression.

1. This steak is ________________. (너무 익었어요)
2. This dish is ________________. (덜 익었어요)
3. The service is ________ ________________. (너무 느려요)
4. This soup is ________ ________________. (너무 짜요)
5. There is ________ ________ ________. (너무 좁아요)
6. This restaurant is ________ ________________. (너무 비싸요)
7. It's ________ ________________. (너무 더워요)
8. It's been ________________. (요금이 너무 비싸게 나왔네요)

Exercise

1. 3명이 앉을 자리가 있을까요?

   ----

2. 창가 쪽 테이블이 있습니다.

   ----

3. 주문하시겠습니까?

   ----

4. 스테이크는 어떻게 구워드릴까요?

   ----

5. 오늘의 Soup은 무엇인가요?

   ----

6. 우리에겐 시간이 좀 필요할 것 같아요.

   ----

7. 빈 접시는 치워주시고 영수증을 가져다 주시겠습니까?

Seek & Find

How to solve :

The words in the list at the bottom of the page are hidden within the grid on the next page. The words may be forward, backward, up, down or diagonal. They're always in a straight line and never skip letters. You may use some letters more than once.

Circle the first and last letter of each word within the grid, join them with a straight line and cross it off the word list.

BISCUITS	HASH	PICKLES
BOOTH	HOT DOG	POTATOES
CHILI	MEATLOAF	RELISH
COFFEE	MILK	SANDWICH
COUNTER	MUFFINS	SAUSAGE
EGGS	MUSTARD	SLAW
FRIES	OATMEAL	SOUP
GRAVY	PANCAKE	SPECIAL
GRILL	PEPPER	STOOLS

P	E	P	P	E	R	S	T	O	O	L	S	L	L
S	T	I	R	G	E	X	M	J	F	L	J	A	L
P	E	B	U	T	T	E	R	I	A	R	E	I	I
H	C	I	W	D	N	A	S	W	L	M	I	C	R
S	H	S	P	R	U	E	B	R	T	K	S	E	G
E	I	C	F	A	O	L	T	A	E	M	L	P	S
L	L	U	H	T	C	T	O	T	S	G	O	S	V
K	I	I	A	S	P	I	C	L	N	C	R	A	M
C	H	T	T	U	I	H	M	O	E	S	O	U	P
I	O	S	O	M	U	L	C	R	F	S	F	S	B
P	T	N	A	P	H	A	E	O	O	F	G	A	R
R	D	E	S	H	B	A	O	R	I	F	E	G	H
B	O	O	T	H	L	P	A	N	C	A	K	E	E
Q	G	N	D	A	N	I	S	H	G	R	A	V	Y

Discussion

What do you think of tipping?

A : Did you know that people in the US and Canada tip at restaurants, airports, and hotels?

B : Yes I do. But we don't tip taxi drivers, hairdressers, or waitress in Korea.

A : **You're right.** What do you think of tipping?

B : Some people like hotel door attendants, parking valets, and hotel maids get low salaries. So, maybe they need tips.

A : You're right. They work hard to please customers because of tips.

B : What would you do if the Korean government asked you to tip at restaurants, hotels, etc?

A : What? I hope not.

팁에 대해 어떻게 생각하는가?

A : 미국이나 캐나다에서는 식당이나 공항, 호텔에서 팁 주는 것을 알고 있나요?

B : 네. 그러나 한국에서는 택시 운전사나 미용사, 식당 종업원들에게 팁을 주지 않지요.

A : **맞아요.** 팁에 대해 어떻게 생각하세요?

B : 호텔에서 문을 열어주거나 주차를 해주는 분 혹은 호텔 관리인들은 낮은 임금을 받잖아요. 그러니까 아마도 팁이 필요할 거예요.

A : 맞는 말이예요. 팁 때문에 고객에게 더 열심히 일할 수도 있을 테지요.

B : 만약 한국 정부가 식당이나 호텔에서 팁을 주라고 한다면 어떻게 하시겠어요?

A : 뭐라고요? 그러지 않길 바랄 뿐이예요.

Tip

You're right. 맞습니다.

상대 토론자의 의견에 동의할 때 쓸 수 있는 표현이다.

- It may be right.
- It's true.
- Sure.
- It's right.
- I think so.

Topics for further discussion

❶ Where do you prefer to eat, at home or out?

❷ What are your favorite top five dishes?

❸ If you introduce Korean food to your customer, what's your top three food and how to explain those?

10

Reading

Sindang-dong : Heaven for 'tteokbokki' lovers

Seoul has plenty of alleys full of mom-and-pop kitchens. Sindang-dong food alley is renowned for tteokbokki, a broiled dish of sliced rice cake, meat, eggs and seasoning. In Jangchung-dong, there are pork hock restaurants. Gongdeok-dong is famous for assorted pan-fried delicacies, while Hwanghak-dong is filled with small broiled beef tripe kitchens. Euljiro is famous for restaurants that specialize in golbaengi muchim – a spicy mix of sea snails, salad and red pepper paste.

Tteokbokki is made by adding on numerous supplementary ingredients to the round shaped rice-cake made of rice. This food is usually sold at street stalls and snack bars, and is one of Korea's favorite snacks. However, tteokbokki was originally one of the royal dishes eaten in January, packed with meat and vegetables, and seasoned with soy sauce instead of Korean hot pepper paste.

Likewise, it was considered a delicacy reserved only for kings – one that ordinary people had only heard about.

The tteokbockki in Sindang-dong has a wide range of tastes. Outlets add ramen, jjclmyeon(wheat noodles), egg, dumplings and fried food to the usual ingredients – rice-cake, fish cakes and Korean hot pepper paste.

There are also variations with seafood, cheese, and curry designed to cater to foreign palates. There is a super-hot taste called "tears tteok-bokki" – it's so hot it will make your eyes water. Along with bibimbab and galbi, tteokbokki is one of the most popular dishes with tourists. There is even a research lab for tteokbokki in Siheung, Gyeonggi Province to focus on the globalization of the dish.

Most of the Sindang-dong tteokbokki kitchens operate 24 hours a day, and offer valet parking. Stores such as "I Love Ddeobokki" (www.ilovesindangdong.co.kr) have DJs that play requested songs. The tteok-bokki stores also serve ice cream, the perfect dessert after a spicy dish.

Getting there : Get off at Sindang Station on Subway Line 2. Go out of Exit No. 4, and walk toward Dongdaemun Stadium Station for about 300 meters, and you will arrive at the Sindang-dong Tteokbokki alley.

(www.koreaherald.co.kr)

케이맨 군도*Cayman lalands*

카리브해의 케이맨 군도는 공기의 오염, 인구의 과밀, 자동차의 소음 등 여러 가지 혼란 가운데 둘러싸여 육체적 또는 정신적으로 매우 피곤한 현대인들이 선호하는 여행 목적지 중 하나이다.

Unit 11

Could you recommend us some good places to go?

11 Could you recommend us some good places to go?

Before we go

- Which of Korea's tourist sites would you recommend to your foreign friends?
- How often do you shop for clothes?
- Where is the best place for shopping in Seoul?

Words and phrases

- sight
- museum
- reasonable price
- entrance fee
- observatory
- fitting room
- particular
- recommendation

City tour (1) CD TRACK 1

Chae-rim :	My friend and I have a few hours free this afternoon and we'd like to go sightseeing. **Could you recommend us some good places to go?**
Staff :	Sure, New York is full of very interesting places to go like museums, markets, famous buildings... do you have any particular interest?
Chae-rim :	We just want to visit a nice place. But we are sure that we would like to go shopping.
Staff :	Certainly, ma'am. Let me show you some brochures. The Empire States Building is only a few minutes from here. The view from the top of The Empire States Building is one of the best in New York. You must see it while you're here. After that, you should go to Farmer's Market for shopping. Farmer's Market is shopper's paradise. You can buy whatever you want with reasonable price.

Chae-rim : Is there any entrance fee for the Empire States Building?

Staff : Yes, $18.45 for the observatory.

Chae-rim : Do you know what time the Empire States Building opens?

Staff : It opens daily, 365 days a year. 8:00 am to 2:00 am, 7 days a week. Last elevators go up at 1:15 am.

Chae-rim : Alright. How about the distance between the Empire States Building and Farmer's market? Is it far from one to another?

Staff : No. It's not. You just pay the minimum cab fare.

Chae-rim : Oh, great. Thank you for your help.

Staff : No problem. Have a nice trip in New York.

City tour (2) CD TRACK 2

Staff : Hello, can I help you?

Tourist : Yes, please. I'm here in Seoul for two days and I would like to see the major sites. Can

	you give me any ideas about what is there to see?
Staff :	Oh, yes, sure. But you can really only see the major sites in two days because there is a lot to see in Seoul. I suggest you have a look at the National Museum and the N Tower, which are marked here on the map.
Tourist :	Are they open today?
Staff :	Yes. Both sites are open today. You can see the major attraction inside the museum, and the night view from the top of the N Tower is just fantastic!
Tourist :	How do I get there from here?
Staff :	Well, if I were you, I would take the bus that stops right out side the building, here. It's number 88 and it also takes you to many of the sites in Seoul.
Tourist :	That sounds very nice. Do I have to buy a special ticket?
Staff :	It's 1,200 won for one trip, and 3,500 won for the one day pass.
Tourist :	Thank you so much. I really appreciate it.

Shopping CD TRACK 3

Clerk: May I help you?

Chae-rim: No, thank you. **I am just looking.**

Clerk: OK. Take your time and let me know if you need any help.

Chae-rim: Sure. Thanks.

(After a few minutes later)

Chae-rim: **May I try this skirt on?** Where is the fitting room?

Clerk: This way, please.

Chae-rim: This one is too small for me. Do you have a larger one?

Clerk: Then, try this. This is larger than that. This skirt fits you well.

Chae-rim: I'll take it. Do you accept credit cards?

Grammar point

비교급

This is larger than that. 이것이 저것보다 크다.

둘 이상의 것을 비교할 때 비교급을 쓴다. 비교급 평서문 형태는 대개 주어+동사+(목적어)+비교급 형용사/부사+than+비교 대상이다. 비교급 형용사/부사는 형용사/부사에 'er'을 뒤에 붙이거나 앞에 'more'를 붙여 만든다.

예를 들어 'tall'의 비교급은 'taller'이고, 'expensive'의 비교급은 'more expensive'이다. "He is taller than his brother.", "I like summer better than winter."와 같은 문장들은 비교급 문장이다.

앞에서 배운 선택의문문의 형태로 비교의문문을 쓰기도 한다.

- Which is bigger, a taxi or a bus?
- Which do you like better, Seoul or Jeju?

Expression

Take your time.

'천천히 하세요, 서둘지 마세요'라는 의미 표현이다. 음식점에서 메뉴를 보고 있는 손님에게 "Take your time."이라고 하면 '천천히 주문하세요'라는 의미가 된다.

Try on.

Try 동사는 '시험삼아 해보다, 입어보다, 신어보다, 먹어보다, 마셔보다'의 뜻으로 두루 쓰여서, "Can I try this cake?" (이 케이크 먹어봐도 될까요?) "I want to try this car before I buy it." (차 구매하기 전에 먼저 시운전을 해보고 싶어요)과 같이 사용된다.

This skirt fits you well.

Fit는 '꼭 맞다, 적합하다'의 뜻으로, 의복과 함께 쓰여 '사이즈 등이 꼭 맞다'라는 의미가 있다. "This coat doesn't fit him." (이 코트는 그에게 맞지 않다)와 같이 쓰인다. 그러나 색상이나 무늬가 어울리다는 뜻으로는 become이나 suit 동사를 쓴다. "바지가 아주 잘 어울리네요"라는 말은 "The pants suit you." 혹은 "You look very well on these pants."로 표현될 수 있다.

Language focus

a little / a few and little / few

(a) little + uncountable noun

(a) little water
(a) little money
(a) little time

- She didn't eat anything, but she drank **a little water**.
- There was **little food** in the refrigerator. It was almost empty.

(a) few + plural noun

(a) few books
(a) few questions
(a) few days

- We're going away **for a few days**.
- There were **few people** in the theater. It was almost empty.

- .... means some but not much and .... means some but not many.
- Both .... and .... mean almost no or almost nothing.
- We use .... and ....with a positive idea, and .... and .... with a negative idea.

Practice

Complete the sentences. Use little/a little/few/a few.

1. There was .... food in the refrigerator. It was almost empty.

2. "When did she go out?" ".................... minutes ago."

3. I can't decide now. I need .... time to think about it.

4. There was .... traffic, so we got there early.

5. Let's take a taxi. There are .... buses after 9 at night.

6. "Would you like more soup?" "Yes, ..., please."

Exercise

1. 실례합니다. 이 노란 스웨터 입어 봐도 될까요?

....

2. 물론이죠. 이리로 오세요.

....

3. 이것은 너무 커요. 더 작은 것 있나요?

....

4. 이것을 입어보세요. 이것이 저것보다 더 작거든요.

....

5. 특별히 관심 있는 것이 있나요?

....

6. 입장료를 내야 되나요?

....

7. 여기서 어떻게 그곳까지 갈 수 있나요?

....

Discussion

Where is the best place to stay when traveling?

A : When I go to a foreign country, I always stay at a hotel in downtown.

B : **How come?**

A : Staying in the downtown area is very convenient. In general, the transportation system in downtown is good and I can visit museums and shopping centers easily.

B : That's understandable.

A : Downtown offers exciting night entertainment such as bars and clubs. **You know.** What do you think?

B : I want to relax when traveling.

A : So, **what is your point?**

B : My point is staying in downtown is too hectic. So, I want to stay outside the city.

여행 중에 머물기 가장 좋은 곳은 어디일까요?

A : 저는 해외여행을 갈 때 항상 번화가에 있는 호텔에서 지내요.

B : **왜요?**

A : 번화가에 있는 것은 편리하니까요. 일반적으로 번화가는 교통이 편리하고, 박물관이나 쇼핑몰에 쉽게 갈 수 있어요.

B : 이해가 가네요.

A : 번화가에는 클럽이나 주점 같은 밤 유흥 거리도 많지요. 당신 생각은 어떠세요?

B : 저는 여행기간 동안 긴장을 풀고 싶어요.

A : **말하려는 바가 무엇이죠?**

B : 제 말은 번화가에 머무는 것은 너무 시끄럽고 복잡하다는 말이예요. 그래서 저는 도심 외곽에서 머물고 싶어요.

11

Tip

How come?

'왜?'라는 뜻으로 'why'와 동일한 표현이지만 쓰임에서 약간 차이점이 있다. 'why'는 의문사로서 의문문을 만들 때 "Why do you think so?(왜 그렇게 생각해요?)"와 같이 의문문의 어순을 가지지만, 'How come'은 "How com you think so?"와 같이 일반 평서문의 어순을 가진다. 그러나 위의 두 문장의 뜻은 동일하며, 일반 회화에서는 '왜?'라는 의미로, 'Why' 대신 'How come?'도 흔히 쓰인다.

You know

별 뜻 없이, 말하는 중간에 간격을 두기 위해 쓸 수 있는 구어 표현이다. 토론에서 자신의 의견을 말하면서 시간적 간격이 필요할 때 쓸 수 있다.

What is your point? 말하려는 바가 무엇인가요?

상대방이 말하려는 의도를 잘 알아차리지 못했을 때 쓸 수 있는 표현이다.

- I' don't get it. 이해를 못했어요.
- I didn't catch your point. 말하려는 바가 무엇인지 이해를 못했어요.
- What do you mean? 무슨 의미예요.

Topics for further discussion

❶ What do you think a visitor in Korea should buy?

❷ Have you ever bought anything you don't need?

쇼핑천국 *Shopping paradise*

쇼핑천국으로 명성이 높은 홍콩은 세계 각국에서 온 관광객들로 항상 분주하다.

Unit 12

I want to check out now.

12

I want to check out now.

Before we go

- What's the best trip in your life?
- How many days do you stay in hotels a year?

Words and phrases

- check out
- make out
- get to
- sign
- lobby
- couple of

Check out (1) CD TRACK 1

Receptionist : Good morning. May I help you?

Chae-rim : Yes, please. **I'd like to check out.** Could you give me the bill?

Receptionist : Certainly, ma'am. May I have your name and room number, please?

Chae-rim : I'm Chae-rim Lee, and the room number is 1001.

Receptionist : You are supposed to leave the hotel tomorrow, aren't you?

Chae-rim : Right. But I told the front desk that my check out date would be today. Is there any problem?

Receptionist : No, not at all, Ms. Lee. Your bill comes to $1115 including tax and service charges. How would you like to pay, ma'am?

Chae-rim : I'd like to pay for it with the credit card that I checked in. You've got the number, right?

Receptionist : Sure. We have it. You're all set to go. Here is your receipt. Was everything Ok?

Chae-rim : Everything was fine. By the way, where can I grab a taxi?

Receptionist : Just get out to the main gate. You can find it easily. Thank you for staying at Monte Hotel. Have a nice trip.

Check out (2) CD TRACK 2

Staff : Are you checking out, ma'am?

Chae-rim : Yes, my room number is 8271.

Staff : Here is your bill, Ms. Lee. How would like to pay?

Chae-rim : I'm going to pay cash for this. Hold on a minute... Could you explain these items on my bill, please?

Staff : Certainly, ma'am. What would you like to know?

Chae-rim : What about these phone calls? I don't remember making any phone calls.

Staff : Let me check your record. It says here that there were 2 phone calls to South Korea on

	the 20th of July.
Chae-rim :	Oh, yes, that's right. I called my friend. But I was on the phone only for a couple of minutes. I can't believe it costs that much.
Staff :	We do have our own satellite dish here at the hotel, which adds to the cost. That is the reason why the phone rate is higher than others.
Chae-rim :	But you should have let customers know about that.
Staff :	I'm so sorry ma'am, but there is nothing I can do with this rate.
Chae-rim :	Alright then, I understand that. I just changed my mind. I'm going to pay with my Mastercard this time.
Staff :	Sure. please sign at the bottom. Here is your receipt. Thank you for staying at the Hilton Hotel.

Late check out

CD TRACK 3

Chae-rim : When is the check out time?

Staff : It's 12 o'clock noon, ma'am.

Chae-rim : I'd like to check-out by 4 pm. Is there any extra charge for it?

Staff : Yes, there is an extra charge for late check-out. If you check-out after 6 pm, there is a day's room charge. If you check-out between 3 to 6 pm, there is 30% of one day's charge.

Chae-rim : How about before 3 pm?

Staff : There is no charge for that.

Chae-rim : Is that right? I will take a note of that. How about a service charge?

Staff : Yes. There is a 10% service charge.

Chae-rim : Okay, please give me a 3 pm check-out. If I need more time, I'll let you know.

Staff : Thank you, ma'am.

Chae-rim : Thanks a lot.

Staff : You're welcome.

Grammar point

Be 동사 과거시제

평서문

I / she / he / it	was in class yesterday.
We / you / they	were in class yesterday.

부정문

I / she / he / it	was not in class yesterday.
We / you / they	were not in class yesterday.

의문문	긍정 대답	부정 대답
Was I / she / he / it in class yesterday?	Yes, you were. / Yes, she / he / it was.	Yes, you weren't / Yes, she / he / it wasn't.
Were We / you / they in class yesterday?	Yes, we were. / Yes, I was. / Yes, They were.	Yes, we weren't. / Yes, I wasn't. / Yes, They weren't.

일반동사 과거시제

평서문

I / you / she/he	studied yesterday.
it / we / they	studied yesterday.

부정문

I / you / she/he	did not study yesterday.
it / we / they	did not study yesterday.

의문문	긍정 대답	부정 대답
Did I study yesterday.	Yes, you did.	No, you didn't.
you	I	I
she/he	she/he	she/he
it	it	it
we	we	we
they	they	they

Expression

Be supposed to ~하기로 되어 있다. ~하기로 기대, 요구되다.

"Sarah is supposed to call me tonight."이라고 하면 그 의미는 "I expect Sarah to call me tonight." (오늘 저녁에 Sarah가 전화할 것을 기대하고 있다)이다. 그러나 'was(were) supposed to'로 쓰이면 '하기로 되어 있던 일이 되지 않았다'는 의미로 많이 쓰인다.

Language focus

also / just / already etc.

We often use these adverbs with the verb in the middle of a sentence.

also *just* *already* *all* *both*

- just/already etc., usually go before the verb.
  Jenny is not here. She just went out.
  Tom is a good swimmer. He also plays basketball and soccer.
- Always/never, etc., go after am/is/are/was/were.
  I've got two sisters. They are both married.
  Is Jenny still here?
- Always/never, etc., to between two verbs(have... been/can... find, etc.)
  The students have all finished their homework.
  I've already seen that movie.

12

Practice

Write the sentences with the words in parentheses( ).

1. They went out. (just) *They just went out.* .
2. Do you work in the same place? (still) .
3. Tim plays the violin. (also) .
4. She started a new job. (just) She .
5. Is Andy here? (already) .
6. I have seen that movie. (already) .

Exercise

1. 체크 아웃 하려고 합니다.
2. 내일 체크 아웃 하시기로 하셨습니다. 그렇지요?
3. 네, 그런데 어제 오늘 나갈 거라고 말씀 드렸습니다. 문제가 있나요?
4. 아닙니다. 계산해 드릴게요.
5. 영수증에 있는 항목에 대해서 설명해 주시겠습니까?
6. 체크 인 때 사용한 신용카드로 계산하고 싶습니다.
7. 추가비용이 있습니다.

Discussion

Is there any sexual discrimination for women working in the hospitality industry?

A: Women are enjoying more and more power these days.

B: Don't jump to conclusions. There is still serious sexual discrimination in the hospitality industry.

A: What are you talking about? Sexual harassment is prohibited by law.

B: **You are entirely missing my point.** I was trying to make a point about sexual discrimination in promotions.

A: Pardon me. Please go on.

B: The number of the female attendants is much more than that of the males. Nonetheless, there are fewer women in executive positions in the airline business.

항공업계의 성차별

A: 요즘 여성들의 파워가 강해지고 있어요.

B: 속단하지 마세요. 환대산업에는 여전히 성차별이 남아 있어요.

A: 도대체 무슨 말씀을 하시는 거예요? 성희롱은 법의로 규제돼 있잖아요.

B: **제 말을 오해하셨네요.** 승진에서의 성차별을 얘기하려던 것이었어요.

A: 미안합니다. 하시던 말 계속하세요.

B: 여 승무원들 수가 남 승무원보다는 많지만, 경영 간부급에 있는 여성은 거의 없어요.

12

Tip

You are entirely missing my point.
제 말을 오해하고 있어요.

토론 시 상대방이 자신의 말을 제대로 이해하지 못할 때 쓸 수 있는 표현이다.

- You have misunderstood my point.
- That's not what I meant.
- That's not I am trying to say.

Topics for further discussion

❶ What would you do if you were overcharged for a long distance call?

❷ Have you ever thought of living in a foreign country for the rest of your life?

❸ Would you rather stay in a room with an extra charge for a late check out or hang around the airport until the departure?

Reading

Guam : the Nearest Paradise Packed With Every Fun

GIANT-GUAN--With the government pushing ahead with the five-day workweek, wage-earners are ending up with more time on their hands – but many people still haven't figured out what to do with the extra leisure hours.

Although Koreans still aren't too familiar with the concept of a weekend-getaway, they certainly are growing fond of the idea of a leisurely trip away.

Guam may be a good option for such a travel.

Located only four hours away by plane, Guam may not be that most exotic place for Koreans. As a matter of fact, it is even less fascinating than most tourist attractions in South Korea.

There is nothing exotic about Guam except the fact that every person one meets on the island will say "Hafa Adai," which means hello in the native Chamorro language.

Being an island of less than 550 square kilometers – bout one third the size of Cheju Island – there are not many places to go there, except a few tourist attractions.

So why should one spend a weekend away in Guam? The real

question is, why shouldn't you?

Guam offers various activities and pleasures from dining, dinner shows, marine sports, golf, sightseeing, family barbeques and sunset cruises.

But it is best known for the diving spots around its cobalt-colored coastline, speaking with coral and exotic fish.

Whatever kind of diving interests one may have – photography, spear fishing, wreck and reef diving, or just a relaxing day admiring tropical fish and coral in crystal clear waters – Guam provides it.

For those who are new to diving, or even swimming all together, one may also take an easy dive at the "Seawalker," where all that's required is to put on a helmet and take a walk across the sea bed.

For visitors seeking less vigorous recreation, Guam may again be the perfect place with dozens of activities including hotel saunas, cock-fights, dog races, baseball or soccer games, shooting galleries, or simply relaxing on one of the island's serene beaches.

More than 40 deluxe hotels have made Guam the perfect place for honeymooners, offering luxury and oceanfront views on their special first nights.

Guam is also a great place for families with children. Ohana Oceanview Guam, one of its most luxurious hotels and an affiliate of the world-famous Outrigger hotel, also offers condominium-style rooms where a family of six may put up comfortably with two bathrooms, a kitchen and two bedrooms, as well as a balcony overlooking one of the island's most beautiful beaches.

Several golf courses designed by great golfers such as Jack Niklaus, Gary Player, and Sam Snead are spread throughout the island.

For shopping crazed visitors, Guam also offers virtually everything and anything free of tax, since the entire island is designated as a duty free zone for visitors.

Also, to add to the list of reasons why Guam is an ideal place for a weekend vacation, Korean Air offers daily flights to Guam, making a three-day vacation over the weekend possible.

One may catch an 8:25 pm flight out of Incheon on Friday after getting off work, and catch a 2:30 am return flight from Guam on Monday morning to be back before the workweek begins at 9:00 am.

(source from travelinfo.co.kr)

기내 면세품 사전 주문

정성이 담긴 작은 선물은 추억을 전할 수 있어 좋으나 선물을 사와야 하는 당사자에게는 엄청난 부담이 아닐 수 없다. 선물의 값이 싸고 비싸고를 떠나서 어떤 물건을 사야 하는가에 대한 고민이 더 큰 것이 사실이다. 이런 부담 때문에 귀국길 공항면세점은 항상 마지막 선물을 사려는 사람들로 북새통을 이루게 마련이고 쇼핑에 정신이 팔려 비행기 출발시간도 잊고 뛰어다니는 해프닝을 간혹 보기도 한다.

이 고민의 해결책으로 기내 면세점을 이용하는 방법이 있는데, 국내 항공사인 대한항공과 아시아나항공은 사전에 원하는 품목을 주문하면 탑승편 기내에서 승무원이 요청한 주문품을 전달해 준다.

이 서비스는 돌아오는 항공편에서 면세품을 받고자 하는 경우에도 이용할 수 있는데 기내에서 예약주문서를 작성해 승무원에게 주면, 돌아오는 기내에서 원하는 물품을 받을 수 있다. 이 귀국편 예약주문은 3일 이후에 출발하는 항공편에 한하여 가능하다. 여행 일정이 짧아 하루나 이틀 정도의 여정이라면 이용이 불가능하다. 이것은 기내 판매품이 면세품이므로 통관절차에 시간이 소요되기 때문이다.

이 서비스를 이용하면 여행 중에 선물을 사기 위해 고민할 필요가 없으며 여행 중에 무거운 선물 꾸러미를 들고 다니지 않아 여행에 여유가 생겨 좋다.

아시아나항공*Asiana Airlines*

항공사의 상품인 좌석은 목적지에 의해 탄생한다.

Unit 13

I don't feel well...

13

I don't feel well...

Before we go

- What would you do if you were lost in a foreign country?
- Do you prefer to take a medicine when you have a headache?

Words and phrases

- pharmacy
- headache/fever
- tablet/medicine
- airsick
- wallet
- lost

At the pharmacy

CD TRACK 1

Chae-rim :	Do you have any medicine for a stomach-ache?
pharmacist :	Yes, we have several kinds. How long have you had the pain?
Chae-rim :	Since yesterday morning. I thought it was something that would just go away easily.
pharmacist :	Have you ever had this kind of trouble before?
Chae-rim :	Yes, but not very often.
pharmacist :	This one will be good for you. Take two tablets 30 minutes after a meal. However, you need to see a doctor if this medicine doesn't make you feel better.
Chae-rim :	Yes, but how much is it?
Clerk :	It's 4 dollars and 37 cents, including tax.
Chae-rim :	Okay. Here is five bucks.
Clerk :	There you are. Here's your change. I hope you feel better soon.
Chae-rim :	Thank you. I'm sure I will.

In case of getting an airsick

CD TRACK 2

Chae-rim : Excuse me. I don't feel well, I think I have a fever. Do you have any medicine?

Flight attendant : Yes. Please wait a minute.
Here is some aspirin and water. You should take two tablets.

Chae-rim : Thank you.

(..............)

Flight attendant : How are you feeling now? Do you need an extra blanket?

Chae-rim : No, it's OK. I feel a lot better now, thank you. Can I just have some more warm water?

Flight attendant : Certainly ma'am. I'll be back with some water.

Chae-rim : Thank you.

Lost wallet

CD TRACK 3

Chae-rim : I lost my travel wallet. I've looked everywhere. I think I've lost it.

Chae-rim's friend : What's in it?

Chae-rim : Cash, credit cards, and an airline ticket. Fortunately, I left my passport in the hotel. I just can't believe that it happened to me.

Chae-rim's friend : **Take it easy** my friend. First of all, you need to call the police and report it. Then, call the bank and let them know that you lost your credit card.

Chae-rim : What about my plane ticket?

Chae-rim's friend : I think you should call the airline and explain what happened, I'm pretty sure that they'll reissue your ticket.

Chae-rim : That's a good idea. Thank you!!

13

Grammar point

제안표현

'~게 어때?'라고 제안하는 표현은 여러 가지다.

How about ~ing?
What about ~ing?
What do you think of ~ing?

} 처럼 동명사를 쓰는 표현도 있으며,

Why don't we~?
Shall we~?
Let's ~.

} 와 같이 동사원형을 쓰는 표현법이 있다.

긍정 대답	부정 대답
That sounds great/good/terrific. I'd like(love) to.	I am afraid not. I'd like to, but I can't.

Expression

take it easy.

'take it easy'는 보통 "서두르지 말고 느긋하게 해.", "화내지 말고 진정해." 등으로 표현되는데 상대방이 성급해 하거나 불안해 할 경우 흥분을 가라앉히고 마음의 평정을 찾으라는 의미로 "진정해." 라는 뜻으로 많이 쓰인다.

Take it easy! Don't panic.
진정해! 겁먹지 마.
The doctor told me to take it easy for a few weeks.
의사가 내게 몇 주 동안 일을 좀 쉬엄쉬엄 하라고 말했다.

Exercise

1. 혹시 두통약 있나요?

2. 여기 있습니다. 식사 후 30분 후에 2알씩 드세요.

3. 지갑을 분실한 것 같아요.

4. 안에 무엇이 들어 있나요?

5. 전에도 이렇게 아프신 적이 있었나요?

6. 나한테 이런 일이 생길 줄이야... 믿어지지가 않네요.

7. 항공사에 전화하셔서 어떤 일이 일어났는지 말씀하세요.

Discussion

Which do you prefer, traveling alone or traveling with a companion?

A : I prefer traveling alone to traveling with other people. I can map out the trip schedule on my own. Besides, I have time to think about my life and myself.

B : My opinion is different from yours. I do believe traveling with a friend during a trip can be a great help. If I got sick, my friend could take care of me. Also, I'll feel much safer with the friend when I am walking at night or sleeping at a cheap hotel.

혼자 여행하는 것과 동료와 함께 여행하는 것 중 어느 것을 선호하나요?

A : 저는 혼자 여행하는 것을 더 좋아해요. 저만의 여행 스케줄을 짤 수 있으니까요. 게다가 삶과 저 자신에 대해 깊이 생각할 충분한 시간도 갖게 됩니다.

B : 저의 생각은 달라요. 저는 친구와 함께하는 것이 큰 도움이 된다고 생각해요. 아플 때 친구가 저를 돌봐줄 수도 있고, 여행 동반자가 있으며 싼 호텔에서 자거나 밤에 거리를 걸어 다녀도 훨씬 안전하니까요.

Tip

Besides 게다가

자신의 주장에 또 다른 근거를 덧붙이고자 할 때 쓸 수 있는 표현이다.

- Additionally
- In addition
- Moreover
- Furthermore
- Plus

Topics for further discussion

❶ Have you ever been lost in a new town? If yes, how did you feel and what did you do?

❷ What are you going to do if you lose your passport?

❸ Do you often catch colds? How do you protect yourself from catching a cold?

Reading

Where to visit in Seoul, a city with soul

Seoul is full of life; a unique city where the present harmonizes with the past. Scattered among ever-expanding business districts packed with high-rise buildings, you will find enriching cultural heritage and historical establishments such as ancient palaces. Seoul is bustling with exciting events and cultural facilities.

Colorful performances and reenactments of traditional activities are commonplace, and with plenty of museums and galleries, the city is full of places to go and see. Seoul is also blessed with natural beauty; the Han River which meanders through the center and magnificent mountains surrounding it. For sports fanatics, we were hosts to the Olympic Games in 1988 and will co-host the World Cup in 2002. The main stream of politico-economic activities run into and out of Seoul. Whether you're looking for amusement, culture or a business opportunity, Seoul is the right place for you.

The more you learn about Korean culture, the happier you will be in Seoul.

(source from travelinfo.co.kr)

TIPS FOR A COMFORTABLE AND CAREFREE FLIGHT

By Dr. Dalbir Singh Sagoo, Senior Aviation Medical Examiner

At Malaysia Airlines, we care for your safety and comfort. For your general inflight well-being, we would recommend the following.

- Be physically and mentally relaxed and enjoy the flight. Do some reading, talking, watch movies or take a nap.
- Wear comfortable clothes, suitable shoes and preferably tights or support stockings.
- Drink adequate water or fruit juices. Avoid too much caffeine and alcoholic beverages which may cause dehydration. Eat a lot of fruits and avoid food high in sodium and salt.
- Avoid prolonged sitting. Walk about when possible. Shake legs once in a while!
- Do the simple in-flight exercises illustrated on this page to exercise the foot, leg, hip and back muscles and improve blood circulation.
- Gentle massaging of the feet, legs, body and arms has beneficial effects.
- If you experience discomfort such as pain and swelling of your legs, rapid or difficulty in breathing, please seek immediate medical attention on arrival.

Have a pleasant flight!

BASIC EXERCISES FOR TRAVELLERS

- Raise your arms so that your elbows form a 90 degree angle at chest level. Press the palms of your hands together. Hold the position for six seconds, relax and repeat five to ten times.

- Sit with one foot flat on the floor close to your chair. Raise the opposite foot five inches off the floor, first flexing and then pointing your toes. This increases circulation in your lower leg and foot muscles. Repeat up to 20 times. Do the same with the other foot.

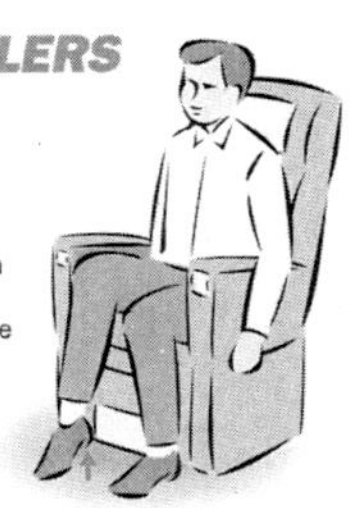

- Tilt your head backwards, arch your back and hold for six seconds, then bring your chin down to rest on your chest. Hold for six seconds, then repeat five to ten times.

- Sit upright on the edge of the couch or chair with your back straight, lift one foot and then the other as if you are marching, bringing your knees high and pumping your arms as you go. Maintain exercise as long as you are comfortable.

- Press both elbows against the seat while keeping your head and chest up and chin in. Breathe normally, hold the contraction for six seconds, then relax. Repeat five times.

일반석 증후군 예방법

비좁은 비행기 좌석에서 움직이지 않고 오랫동안 앉아 있을 경우 다리 정맥에 혈전(血栓 : 혈관 안에서 피가 엉겨 굳은 덩어리)이 생겨 혈구의 흐름을 막음으로써 호흡곤란 등을 일으키는 현상을 일반석 증후군이라 하며, 이코노미석 증후군이라고도 한다. 이러한 증상을 예방하기 위한 운동법이다.

조인환 Cho, Inhwan
Professor of Tourism Division, Baekseok Arts University

심성우 Sim, Sungwoo
Professor of Tourism Division, Baekseok Arts University

김지회 Kim, Jihoe
Professor of Tourism Division, Baekseok Arts University

English for Hospitality and Tourism
(MP3 CD 포함)

2010년 3월 5일 초판 1쇄 발행
2018년 1월 26일 초판 5쇄 발행

지은이 조인환 · 심성우 · 김지회
펴낸이 진욱상
펴낸곳 백산출판사
교 정 편집부
본문디자인 편집부
표지디자인 오정은

저자와의 합의하에 인지첩부 생략

등 록 1974년 1월 9일 제406-1974-000001호
주 소 경기도 파주시 회동길 370(백산빌딩 3층)
전 화 02-914-1621(代)
팩 스 031-955-9911
이메일 edit@ibaeksan.kr
홈페이지 www.ibaeksan.kr

ISBN 978-89-6183-257-1
값 15,000원